Royalty Meets Enneagram

Understanding Personality Style 7: Meghan Markle, Sarah Ferguson Princess Tessy

JANICE SETO

Royalty Meets Enneagram: Understanding Personality Style 7
Meghan Markle, Sarah Ferguson, Princess Tessy

http://janiceseto.wix.com/words
amazon.com/author/janiceseto
www.janiceseto.com

Copyright © 2018 Janice Seto

All rights reserved. No portion of this book (including content, illustrations, images) may be reproduced in any form without expressed permission from the publisher. For permissions, contact Janice Seto

ISBN-13: 978-1-926935-36-2 (printed)
ISBN-13: 978-1-926935-37-9 (electronic)

DEDICATION

Janet
Brends
Debs
Pat
Joy
David
Dr Liz
Dr LA

Gail

CONTENTS

DEDICATION iv
CONTENTS vi
ACKNOWLEDGEMENTS ix
Preface to the Series: Royalty Meets Enneagram 1
1. Who wants to be a Princess? 6
2. The Firm & Its Bureau-stocracy 14
    A.   The Firm: Business as usual, Status Quo 16
    B.   HR is not your friend: Bait N Switch 21
        i.   HR Fail: Talent walks out the door 23
        ii. The Firm's dilemma: Shift or Go Extinct 25
3. She's got Personality 30
    A.   The Enneagram Personality System 33
        i.   Overview 34
        ii. Royalty meets Enneagram 39
    B.   Princess Enneagram Personality Type by Shoe Styles ... 41
4. Enneagram 7: The Promoter 43
    A. Her Strengths 46
        i.   All over the World 47
        ii. We're here for a good time, not a long time… 49
        iii. Fun fun fun 51
    B.   Her Challenges 53
        i.   Ghosting: Someone I used to know 55
        ii. Curb Your Enthusiasm: Livin' la Vida Loca 58
        iii. Reinventing: Raindrops keep fallin on my head 62
        iv. Uninhibited Rebel: Grease is the word 64
    C.   Enneagram 7 Promoter Shoe: Gladiator Stiletto 69
5. Enneagram 7 Promoter: Subtypes 71
    A.   Focus on The One: Intimate Subtype 72
    B.   Focus on The Few: Self-Preservation Subtype 74
    C.   Focus on The Many: The Social Subtype 78
6. Enneagram 7 Promoter Princess: Prison or Paradise? 81
    A. Sarah Ferguson: Don't Make Me Over 81
    B. Princess Tessy: Is That All There Is? (No!) 84
    C. Meghan Markle: Con Te Partiro 88
7. Enneagram for Happily Ever After 94
REFERENCES IN THE SERIES 108

References in Enneagram 7 Promoter Princess............................ 112
ABOUT THE AUTHOR.. 144

ACKNOWLEDGEMENTS

Thank you to the most wonderful reviewers,
I deeply appreciate your time and interest.

Eka for assistance on the book series cover.

Lynn Roulo, author of Headstart for Happiness: Enneagram and Kundalini

Janet Stucken Haigh, who introduced me to the Enneagram

Tessy Antony de Nassau, Princess of Luxembourg

Sister Patricia Shreenan, first among the Enneagram teachers offering sessions all over the world

Gail who encouraged me
despite wondering what in the world
I have gotten myself into now

Preface to the Series: Royalty Meets Enneagram

I have been researching for this series for over a decade and am now able to start publishing this 9-part series on the Enneagram and royalty.

The latter has been of interest since Mrs (Joan) Anyan spoke to our primary class about a royal tour starting in Canada. She caught our attention with the British monarchy's anachronistic line of succession to the Crown with the fact of male primogeniture (changed in 2013). That was her answer to our voluble questions why Princess Anne and her descendants follow her younger brothers, Prince Andrew and Prince Edward.

Later on, in high school, I started the complete family tree of descendants from Prince Albert and Queen Victoria. (This dates me as pre-Google, as nowadays I would just refer to the research of Marlene Eilers Koenig http://royalmusingsblogspotcom.blogspot.com/ .)

My introduction into the Enneagram personality typology is slightly more recent, via a flatmate, Janet Stucken, now the respected teacher and examiner in the International Baccalaureate. In those pre-Yahoo days, the canons of the Enneagram were available only by searching through bookstores and the occasional library – Helen Palmer, Kathy Hurley & Ted Dobson, Suzanne Zuercher, Don Riso & Russ Hudson, Margaret Frings Keyes, Michael Goldberg, Jerome Wagner, Elizabeth Wagele, Katherine Fauvre, David Fauvre, Richard Rohr.

These early Enneagram writers by and large made the typology accessible to all who seek to deepen their self-awareness and kept seminar and training costs to a minimum. Through their collective generosity, I join the many who could attend sessions with Sister Patricia Shreenan, Michael Goldberg, Kathy Hurley and Ted Dobson (Theodorre Donsson), Helen Palmer and David Daniels, Jerome Wagner, and also meet Don Riso and Russ Hudson at the International Enneagram Association's annual conference in Toronto. All these were elements in my own research and later dissertation.

Information about royalty, however, remained too closely held in 2008 when I did started my research on both royal figures and their Enneagram personality types, and so I put this book on hiatus.

A decade later, I am picking up where I left off. Today's internet technology is more open to research and data mining from most locations through the world. More people are reading and researching and sharing the Enneagram in what I would call the second wave of writers. Monarchies are more open with official social media updates and photos. The Firm, as the British Monarchy is commonly known, is getting ahead of traditional media to deliver information directly to the populace.

Sister Patricia Shreenan is very clear, cautioning against 'typing' someone else's personality. It is very presumptuous to buttonhole others, pigeonhole their personality, and give unsolicited advice. Mindful of that, this book series is written from an organizational psychology perspective. Businesses, charities, NGOs have missions and goals and targets to meet; they need staff with skills. More importantly, there must be a 'fit' between the prospective candidate and the job and the organization.

Ultimately, the organization wants to screen, interview, and hire on a probationary basis someone with the humility to learn and work well with other people. The 'bad hire' is the unfortunate term for a 'misfit' or a 'poor fit' between the new employee and the organization The organization sometimes hires and expects the new employee to conform quickly to the extant culture. In other situations, the new hire has been taken on precisely to shake things up and change the culture, and ensure the organization's survival. It is often not the employee's fault but failure of the organization to articulate their expectations when there is a parting of the ways.

An example of the latter is the professor of psychology, Robert J Sternberg. He almost had his life totally upended after starting his work as president of the University of Wyoming with the goal to make change happen quickly. Unfortunately, enough influential stakeholders disliked his pace and style, and there was a mutual parting of the ways (Sternberg, 2014).

It is in the best interest of the prospective hire, the organization, and the work ahead that I offer this series of insights into the 9 different Enneagram personality styles. To get new hires oriented and able to hit the ground running these days is beyond the HR department simply handing them a manual. Ideally, it is a shared dynamic throughout the organization.

To illustrate each of the 9 Enneagram personality styles, I have drawn from royal personages themselves. Today's modernizing monarchies allow their members to speak less from prepared notes and to banter unfiltered. How they speak extemporaneously in interviews and interact with the public, their actions hint at underlying motivations. And it is through the lens of their motivations that Royals shine a spotlight onto personality.

In this book, Enneagram 7 Promoter Princess, I refer to Meghan

Markle, Sarah Ferguson, and Tessy Antony de Nassau Princess of Luxembourg as exemplars of this personality style. Sarah Ferguson has been cited as a 7 by author Riso & Hudson, Michael Goldberg, Katherine Fauvre and David W Fauvre, among other Enneagram researchers. By observation, I would agree all three women exhibit behaviours and motivations that strongly indicate Enneagram personality 7, a style that tends to be given a 'bad rap' for a poor marital track record. All three women have called time on their first marriages. I would assert in this book instead that their examples are actually positive role models of Enneagram 7 Promoter Princess:

1. Why Meghan and Harry have the setup to succeed
2. How Sarah and Andrew couldn't catch a chance at marriage
3. Where Princess Tessy is heading

This book is divided into three parts that you are free to read out of order: a short primer on The Firm's organizational effectiveness, an short overview of the Enneagram, and an examination of personality style 7 with examples from the lives of these royal women. At the end of the book is a list of references for anyone interested in pursuing a deeper understanding of the Enneagram personality typology.

Royalty meets Enneagram: Understanding Personality Style series gives each number a name and a distinct style of shoe that most closely matches her personality.

1 – The Enforcer (pumps/court shoes)

2 – The Compassionate Helper (ballerinas)

3 – The Worker Bee (slingbacks)

4 – The Unforgettable (kitten heels with appliques)

5 – The Investigator (Oxfords)

6 – The Loyal Defender (peeptoes)

7 – The Promoter (gladiator stilettos)

8 – The Boedicia (boots)

9 – The Consensus Builder (mules)

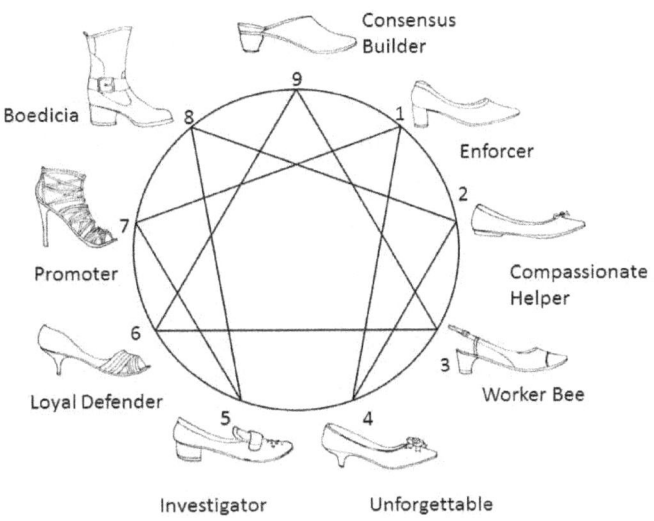

Let's step ahead…

1. Who wants to be a Princess?

Parents, do not wait til she goes to school to encourage your daughter to pursue a career in the STEM professions! If you delay, Disney will get to her first. In 2008, the number one career choice of girls 5 years old is "I want to be a princess" according to a poll by The Children's Mutual. (Carteedge, 2008)

What a success for Disney's Princess marketing strategy – they have now successfully sold action figures, books, and videos of movies and their straight-to-DVD sequels under one umbrella - bundling all their princesses into a convenient package for little girls (and their friends and families) to purchase (Hains, 2016). In the myriad of Disney princesses, little girls also admire royal women who are brave (Snow White), clever (Princess Jasmine), kind (Aurora the Sleeping Beauty), and go about independently, travelling and exploring (Princess Ariel, *The Little Mermaid*). And when necessary, she can 'man up' to take care of her people (Pocahontas).

Moreover, Disney stories sell the story to commoner girls that she can be a princess just by being 'nice girls' like Cinderella and Belle in *Beauty & The Beast* who married into royalty. These commoners did not have any training – they just had to be themselves. Proactive and kind, the new princess is active and makes a difference to everyone. And the court and the commoners and most of all, her new prince and family love her "just the way you are" as Billy Joel would sing.

And when marriages do happen for reasons of state, by the luck of the draw, Princess Aurora and her Prince Philip are already in love anyways in *The Sleeping Beauty*. A love match, not a marriage of convenience - Fate is remarkable, isn't it?

To further smooth the path of true love in Disney movies, bad things do not happen, romance-wise, to princesses. And everywhere in the fairy tale are friendly animals and helpful, cheerful servants and household staff in beautiful palaces. Nor does the new young princess let being famous get to her head.

Besides the clothes and the glamour, today's young girls first and foremost see a handsome young prince who falls in love with someone as ordinary as she is. The prince is smitten and makes her his princess bride. He is intelligent, not boring, has no exes lurking in the background, is childless, and the royal couple does not have onerous royal duties. No intrusive paparazzi buzz around so they can move about freely like Prince Eric and two-legged Princess Ariel in *The Little Mermaid*.

The modern-day Cinderella story movie *Pretty Woman* gave Julia Roberts her big starring role. Its popularity is a sign that many women do not outgrow their attraction to the fairy tale.

<u>Closet Royal Watchers: Girls and Women; Boys to Men</u>

Even men appreciate the appeal of meeting a princess and marrying into royalty. Perhaps not for the romance but for the role she plays in war and leadership fiction. In the *Star Wars* saga, creator George Lucas introduces smart, feisty, blaster-proficient, senator Princess Leia Organa, a modern day. Emotionally disciplined, Leia unleashes a volley of insults at General Tarquin without resorting to vulgarity. She sneers at his 'foul stench', much more effective than calling him a 'sh#t bag'.

Devotees of Star Trek find the logical Vulcans had a system of nobility. In the movie *Star Trek V*, the audiences meet the overemotional Sybok, the older half-brother of Mr Spock, from their father's first marriage to a Vulcan princess.

First world countries that promote schooling for all now see a generation of independent, educated young women entering public life. Gender studies have shown that all-girls schools tend to produce graduates with the highest degree of self-confidence. Perhaps it is because they get attention and appreciation without competing with those attention hogs AKA boys. Regardless, more and more women everywhere see the glass ceiling as an irksome but surmountable obstacle to career and social mobility.

A sign that social mobility drives important family decisions - many parents select their high achieving child's educational institutions for the prestige and networking opportunities rather than strictly educational quality. The British public school system has done this for centuries as which selective, often independent, fee-paying school dog whistles where someone attended (Sherborne vs the local comprehensive) is like a dogwhistle in, using the words of Jade Jodelle, 'the fetid British Class system' (Joddle, 2015). In France, to attend one of the Grandes Ecoles means access to the ultimate black book for career advancement in the French civil service. On the campuses of many North American universities, fraternities and sororities with their clubby names like Phi Beta Kappa or Skull & Bones are infamous for hazing during initiation rush week.

In the 21st century, research universities are academic powerhouses attracting the best and the brightest - all the way from undergraduate to post-doctoral studies – who, regardless of background, can mingle at the gym, free lectures, political clubs, student media, and the library.

Nobility and royal status in real life can be aspired to and achieved - not just married into or born into - and is within reach. The Roman

Caesars, Corsican Napoleons, and the Karageorgivcs in the Balkans, the Savoys in Italy, Tudors in England, and the Stewarts of Scotland all fought and schemed their way to thrones. In Malaysia, the king is a rotating position among the different heads of seven states in the federation. Art follows reality with the prequel trilogy to *Star Wars*. Thirty years later after Star Wars, George Lucas opened *The Phantom Menace* by introducing the precocious teen – and future mother of Luke Skywalker and Princess Leia - as serving a term as <u>elected</u> queen of the Naboo. In the subsequent two films in the prequel trilogy, the former queen returns to her former status and there is no shame in abdication or retirement or moving on to another career.

Theorizing that a subset of the general population is innately gifted with superior and benevolent leadership qualities has always appealed to people looking outside themselves for leadership. Plato wrote of recognizing the benefits of searching early on for people with "The Right Stuff" and then training them for their sole role in life: leading a government for all.

The key traits of natural-born leaders, many people hoped, would be manifested early enough for the state to spot the talent and put them on a specialized training track. One important marker of talent that is most easily evident is a set of achievements on the 'field'. For the early Tudors, it was battlefield. For Napoleon Buonaparte, it was strategy and political guile.

If leadership qualities are transmitted genetically and the role of leader is inherited, then it would a matter of state for "like to marry like". A married leadership couple would mentor and nurture another generation of people with The Right Stuff in the ultimate apprenticeship environment. Hence the idea of a ruling family in which Nature is Nurtured.

Most countries that eliminate a hereditary monarchy end up creating their own orders of quasi nobility. The Order of Canada with its three levels (Member, Officcr, Companion) is not that different from the United Kingdom's OBE, CBE, KBE, and the orders of Merit in the US. New Zealand as of 2009 is permitting people to use their knighthoods (Sir and Dame) in public. (Barrowclough, 2009) The thinking seems to be that what good is an OBE or OC when you cannot stick a Dame or Sir in front of your name? The standard for admission to these orders has loosened up so now sport stars, fashionable figures, popular culture personalities, business gamechangers like Sir Jony Ives of Apple (Apple Inc, 2018), and music icons like the Bee Gees's Sir Barry Gibb get the nod (Cohen, 2017).

Australia brought theirs back and recanted within a year – as it was poorly rolled out. (Norman & Iggulden, 2015)

As we all know, Napoleon sought to found his own dynasty, by combining his arriviste name with that of a Habsburg bride, Archduchess Marie Louise of Austria. The present head of the Bonaparte family, [Jean-Christophe Napoleon](), has a Borbon Dos Sicilias princess as a mother and Belgian princess as a great grandmother. Through Princess Clementine of Belgium, he is a descendant of Bourbon kings of France and Leopold I, the Coburg uncle to Victoria and Albert. A French general of Napoleon's ended up as King of Sweden and his Bernadotte dynasty similarly gained respect by marrying over the years a representative of the ancient Swedish Wasa royals, various German families, British princess Margaret of Connaught, and Scandinavian counterparts.

A quick scan of the news alerts political junkies for budding media-savvy leaders. Just as New Age healing arts including Reiki talk about a lineage from the founder, leaders and wannabees make use of name recognition and for the tribe they hail from – ie Arnold Schwarzenegger had been married to Maria Shriver, niece of the late president Kennedy; Nelson Mandela came from Xhosa tribe, US President Barack Obama's father was a member of the Luo in Kenya. One of Obama's Chicago advisors, Valerie Jarrett, is from a long line of prominent African-Americans.

Before every US presidential election, genealogists trace how closely the candidates are to the British monarch. More often than not, the one who is more closely related wins.

That defender of the republic, Napoleon Buonaparte, reached back to the Roman republic to Julius Caesar and his great nephew and heir, Octavian/Augustus for his status as First Consul, and later, as Emperor. Napoleon re-created a glittering French court and conferred hereditary titles of his own, to the military, useful people like diplomat Talleyrand, and his family members. To this day, the French Republic allows its citizens to hold titles, legitimate or not, refusing to get involved in genealogical disputes.

Occasionally false claims embarrassingly come to light when a royal enters the picture. The consort of Queen Margrethe of Denmark, the late Prince Henrik, had been commonly known as Count Henri Laborde de Monpezat – however, genealogists found that the family ennoblement did not actually happen, due to the French Revolution and thus their use of the title is in dispute.

Similarly, in the British royal family, matters came to light at the 2004 engagement announcement of Lord Nicholas Windsor to his fiancée, who had been born the aristocratic Paola Doimi De Lupis. In 2000, her entire family changed their surname to the more prestigious "Doimi de Frankopan", despite having little claim to the Croatian royal Frankopan name. This formalized her family's self-transformation from aristocrat to the gradual adoption of the style and mantle of Croatian princes starting in 1991 when the Iron Curtain crumbled. (Palmo, 2006)

The argument used by Paola's family is that with the Frankopan family dying out and that surname no longer used, that it was up for grabs by antecedent branches. It is like Prince Ernst August of Hanover, husband of Princess Caroline of Monaco, stating that he would now be known as a Royal Stuart, since the Hanovers, like the English Stuarts, descended from the Tudors.

Toronto-based Harlequin Books, formerly known for publishing sweet romances from authors including Betty Neels, has capitalized on the large sales of their prince-and-commoner romance titles with more of the same. As in 2018 in anticipation of the wedding of Prince Harry and American actress, Meghan Markle, in 2009, their Mills & Boon imprint issued a series with prince-meets-commoner theme. A decade ago, it added a twist with a fairy tale-meets-sports page and home-team-win-headline-news item. *The Prince's Waitress Wife* by Sarah Morgan, became the first in a special series written for rugby's Six Nations. A wealthy Rugby groupie, Prince Casper, makes the moves on virgin room service waitress, Holly, as she delivers his order to his room. So overwhelmed by mutual passion, they commence to vigorously tryst, a scene described in lurid detail, with the more innocuous bits captured onto the jumboscreen at Twickenham!

It may be an adult version of a fairy tale but fairy tale it definitely is. However, in reality, emotions rarely are the sole reason for the choice of a marriage partner for a royal.

In real life, the love of a prince is hardly enough to result in a royal carriage ride from a wedding. For every Princess Mette-Marit of Norway, there was only a faded hope for a Princess Eva (Miss Sannum for Spain), a Princess Emma (Miss Pernald for Sweden) or a Princess Katja (Miss Katja Storkolm Nielsen in Copenhagen) or a Princess Cressida (Miss Bonas). The trade-off of independence living for a lifetime under scrutiny is unthinkable for these women.

The reverse – a prince who marries someone he is not in love with - is unfortunately true too. Princes themselves may settle for a marriage to someone for whom they have no great passion. On June 1, 2001, the crown prince of Nepal took a gun to his family when he was denied permission to marry a woman he was in love with, who was from a rival family, and was constantly pressured to select from more acceptable noblewomen. Many women would refuse to marry a prince who is in love with someone else - the trade-off of independence living for a life with an unfeeling partner sounds risible in this day and age.

The turbulent marital drama for Charles & Diana had been foreshadowed in his infamous response at the engagement interview, "Whatever love is…"

2. The Firm & Its Bureau-stocracy

George VI aptly called the royal family, The Firm, which indicates the extent to which the institution of monarchy has become professionalized. The late king saw his own staff become unionized and later his elder daughter, the present Queen Elizabeth II, has had to answer to Parliament for everything from the accounts to the determination of market-rents for grace-and-favour apartments. Extending the business metaphor, the royal family are the board of directors of The Firm known as The House of Windsor. The Firm's mission is Survival. Helping set goals and targets are the royal court's executive team and administrative staff, known as the bureaucracy.

Notoriously stingy, the British royal family bureaucrats tend to come from the aristocracy, or as I would call it, the bureau-stocracy. The Royals surround themselves with those that the particular royal personage was comfortable with day –in and day-out. From birth, the Royals live in protective bubbles of private hospitals, independent schools, to the extent that they do not meet nor mix with ordinary people. In short, it makes sense that their staff is largely those with sufficient wealth and background to finance living in London on a courtier's meagre salary. It is all-too-rare that a superb advisor of the calibre of Lord Charteris, the late eminent private secretary to Her Majesty, emerges from the social elite!

Sadly, too often these uninformed courtiers had exerted undue influence that prevents the monarchy from responding appropriately or being proactive in matters that affect its standing with the people upon whom it depends for its survival. These courtiers are limited in being neither effective generalists nor department specialists with up-to-the-minute information. Moreover, those hired for their connections, not their competence – *Who* you know versus *What* you know – in turn hired likeminded people who just happened to be even also lower on the competence scale and so on and so on. When that happens, according to Guy Kawasaki, Steve Jobs of Apple called it 'the bozo explosion'. (Kawasaki, 2011) It is no wonder that the royals develop a reputation for being intractably 'out of touch'.

A British example is the inept and old-fashioned approach to Charles, The Prince of Wales, the heir apparent. Their main mistake was not working with what you have but trying to mould his image. He was marketed as Action Man in his bachelor years, especially in the 1970s. But the Prince of Wales is at his happiest, at his best, when he is engaged in thoughtful discourse and change. Looking back, the chattering classes ridiculed the Prince of Wales's supposedly backwards-thinking on architecture and his support for a sustainable environment. The criticisms seem based on how at odds his interests were to the Action Man brand. Stripping away the 'His Royal Loopiness' backlash, the Prince of Wales is the original, Al Gore came later. His concern with the use of physical space and placement of objects in the environment we would now call feng shui. Over time Charles's positions have been legitimated by more and more people. He has been misunderstood because the courtiers originally went about it all wrong.

No chinless wonder courtier could have accomplished what Mark Bolland later did to rehabilitate Charles's standing with the public after Diana, Princess of Wales's death (Tweedie, 2005). The cunning PR consultant had been entrusted by the Prince of Wales to securing his goal of marriage to Mrs. Camilla Parker Bowles without jeopardizing Charles's claim to the throne. In his public relations analysis, Bolland decided his best shot was to humanize Camilla, a woman the people had demonized as the coldblooded homewrecker who drove Princess Diana into depression and bulimia. As such, he directed Camilla to support osteoporosis charity work, as her own mother suffered from the bone-degeneration disease.

Another part of the rolling-out of the campaign included the message that Camilla did wonders for Charles's temperament. There was too much water under the bridge to hope people would accept Camilla so Bolland did not expend political capital in a lost cause; instead he focused on many people's common experience of putting up with a family member's latest wife. His spin concentrated on making Camilla at least tolerable.

As Charles discovered, Royal houses that seek the best advice, not just insider advice, can survive even his predilection for Camilla.

A. *The Firm: Business as usual, Status Quo*

Until 2002, the British monarchy carried on with the attitude of 'business as usual', with an adherence to the traditional Status Quo way of doing things. Queen Elizabeth the Queen Mother, as long as she was alive, she represented stability and all that was good and traditional. There was no place for creative disruptions like Charles marrying Camilla. If anyone who did not meet the standard was filtered out of the hiring pool.

In the field of organizational behavior, researchers Quinn & Rohrbaugh proposed the Competing Values Framework in analyzing organizational effectiveness (Quinn & Rohrbaugh, 1983). Along two dimensions, degree of control and extent of orientation to the external environment, they proposed that the resultant four quadrants correspond to four models of organization and management. The Firm that Lady Diana Spencer and Sarah Ferguson joined was inner-focused with a high degree of Control – the culture of the Internal Process Model being supported throughout the bureau-stocracy from household staff to courtier and especially to the board members in the interest of maintaining the Status Quo.

All monarchies – save, perhaps Liechtenstein – face a severe staffing shortage. To borrow a filmmaking term, they are short on Talent. In sports, not a very deep bench (Barrett, 2010) With their numerous behind-the-scenes staffers are largely behind the times. The Scandinavians are the skimpiest due to large numbers of morganatic marriages and decreasing fecundity. The Danish have only the descendants of Queen Margrethe II as her sisters's children are excluded. Norwegians are down to three in the line of succession behind Harald V – his son and two grandchildren with daughter Princess Marte Louise renouncing her rights. Carl Gustav of Sweden has only his three children and their offspring – after him.

Even where there is no shortage, the majority in succession to Elizabeth II are in the chorus line. The number of 'headliners' or the core HRH executives – ready to take over - are kept deliberately small to avoid straining the public purse.

The knee-jerk reaction to a staffing shortage by the courtiers is R&R – Recruitment and Retention – is to line up a conventional replacement. A PYT – Pretty Young Thing – naturally captures favourable public attention and brings the promise of a new generation of royals. Soap operas and serials do the same – think of the number of times a new character with a mysterious background struts into the cast of Coronation Street or any serial that had 'Jumped The Shark' and was sliding downhill in popularity.

Like many firms, royal households see a new recruit princess as a turnaround artist plugging a hole in the ranks. She is the savior of the Status Quo. When the environment is static and predictable, as long as the Queen Mother was alive, maintaining order is the main focus, the Internal Process Model.

In this HR-lite scenario, the personnel or HR department follows a simple four-stage process:

1. advertise a posting, listing the criteria and emphasizing the benefits and salary
2. shortlist candidates
3. conduct interviews, and notify the winning candidate
4. schedule an orientation session and present her immediate work assignments

Stage 1 usually is taken for granted, with the media stirring up buzz. The media also helps with Stage 2, acting like headhunters in compiling a list of 'the usual suspects.'

Make no mistake, the royal household - and court supporting the monarchy - steer its royals towards certain choices. It is a very public personnel choice by a Royal Human Resources department based on where the Firm sees itself vis-à-vis the viability of the country and as a healthy organization. The royal courts shop around in the traditional way for a new princess by educating the lad with the right sort of people and surround him with suitable candidates. And cross their fingers that propinquity will result in a successful hire from this casting call.

When she accepts the new role, the new hire gets an HR orientation, usually a quick walk around the premises and a stop with a personnel officer. Most people find this the most interesting part of orientation – completing forms for automatic salary payment deposited directly into bank accounts, benefits explained in detail on extended health care, life insurance, union membership, access to fitness facility.

For a princess-wannabee, the benefits are visible to all. A life of privilege in that she is free from household budgeting, cooking, fighting to get the children into good schools. A life with her swain. And access to the best health care and fitness facilities with an indexed pension upon retirement.

Often, nothing else beyond the rudimentary is done in T&D. Learn the language, keep your mouth shut, be loyal to the man who got you here. They are expected to play a leading role and to be a Star. But do not eclipse the main attraction, the Headliner, as they say in Vegas. The royal prince feels his resentment at being sidelined (Troy-Pryde, 2017). Something that may be inevitable and he should get over, as Sandy Henney, former press secretary for the Prince of Wales says on the documentary Reinventing the Royals: "If you've got a middle-aged, balding man and an incredibly beautiful princess, it's a no-brainer as to who's going to get the media coverage." (BBC, 2015)

Unfortunately, the Status Quo (Inner Process Model) was not universally appreciated by outsiders. The media, for example, had wanted a new 'breath of fresh air' like Sarah Ferguson and Lady Diana Spencer **(Female First, 2017)** to change the traditional Firm, perhaps remain inner-focused but lightening the degree of Control and becoming more Flexible, a more in-tune version of The Firm at formal events (Human Relations Model). On the other hand, the ordinary Briton was in favour of a tightly-controlled message but expansion from traditional pursuits and charities to emerging needs such as AIDS awareness and a land-mine ban (Rational Goal Model). Taking the opposite of Status Quo is ultimate flexibility and unabashed focus on the external environment, The Open Systems Model, the institution of monarchy untethered from a formal role in government. The [Romanian royals](.) (Aanmoen, 2018) and the Orléans and [Napoleon](.) families (Salens, Le prince Jean-Christophe Napoléon aux Invalides, 2018) in France are examples of this Open Systems Model.

Another way of understanding the Competing Values Framework is to look at the various screen adaptations of *Pride and Prejudice* by Jane Austen. If you expect to see *Pride and Prejudice* exactly the way Jane Austen wrote it, then you want the Status Quo, the Internal Process model, as an audience member you want no mucking around with perfection. You would be satisfied with the traditional and conventional BBC 1995 television series. Other filmed versions of *Pride and Prejudice* receive differing opinions. Those who want modern update of Pride and Prejudice are going to appreciate the straight-from-the-book treatment version much less (swimming Mr Darcy notwithstanding) and would be receptive to only one Bingley sister, a divorced Darcy, or an American Darcy (gasp!)

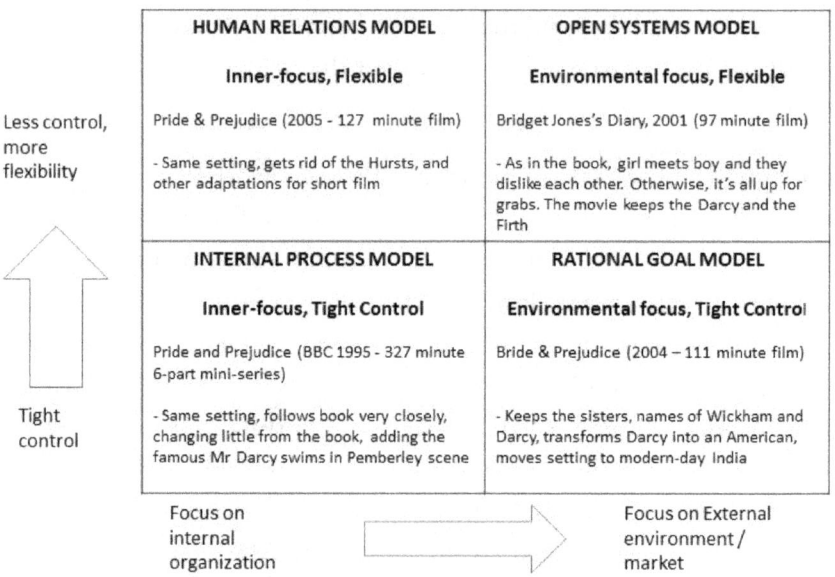

Changing from the Internal Process Model means opening up the wallet. A strategic update of the monarchy includes changing its approach to HRM, Human Resources Management. In light of renewed focus on Human Resources Management at the executive level with mentoring and executive coaching, regardless of which system it adapts ie Human Relations Model or Rational Goal Model or Open Systems Model, the organization of monarchy is too vulnerable for ad hoc or worse, hands-off, attitude towards recruitment and retention and training and development of newcomers.

All firms agree that their most valuable assets are its people, but in tough economic times, cutting its ranks through pink slips is the common knee-jerk reaction. HR serves the employer, The Firm, and will act swiftly to protect it. (Zillman & Fry, 2018) Rather than insufficient training or mentoring or coaching being seen as the cause of 'hiring fail', too often blame is attributed to 'bad fit' of the new recruit.

This happens due to HRM being under-appreciated and de-valued by the finance and operations types in the fierce competition for corporate resources and attention. In order to keep HRM out of the inner Cabinet (meetings of the senior courtiers with the sovereign and royal family members), territorial numbers-crunchers make sure that key decision-makers get fed the impression that HRM is solely concerned with hiring and firing. Hardly worthy of a seat at the table, which would be the natural outcome of . What is left - an *HRM-lite* approach to the people in the workforce - ignores the discipline's rich contributions to a potentially greater and more nimble firm.

B. *HR is not your friend:* Bait N Switch

With fiancées ailed as a 'breath of fresh air', princes marrying outside royal or aristocratic circles seems to indicate that the Firm is relaxing its tight control over the internal (Inner Process Model) to invite flexibility (Human Relations Model). Hopes are high among the populace that her energy, perspective, and ideas portend a renewal and revitalization of the Firm.

Anyone from a non-royal background is in effect a diversity hire. In fall 2006, Prince Louis of Luxembourg married army corporal Tessy Antony, who was an original choice in at least three areas: the first Luxembourg citizen to marry into the Grand Ducal family, the first serving member of the Luxembourg army, and the first native speaker of the national language, Lëtzebuergesch. Also known as Luxembourgish, national language classes for young and old is contributing to its revival (Rankin, 2017). Other outside-the-box royal brides include the divorced journalist Letizia Ortiz Rocasolano, single mother Mette Marit Tjessem Høiby, divorced American actress Meghan Markle.

One must keep in mind that it is usually the external media that calls her 'a breath of fresh air', whereas the courtiers may call her 'young enough to mold' (Inner Processes Model). Ominous signs ahead of that old classic Bait N Switch, if this is indeed the case.

Sarah Ferguson had thought she would live on a naval base in marriage quarters with her husband, Prince Andrew Duke of York, but it turned out she was overruled. Worse, the new HRH The Duchess of York was abandoned to Buckingham Palace and the inhospitable courtiers – what an odd wedding present. She was told to fall in line with the culture. Her training was 'sink or swim'. In her books and interviews, Sarah relates that her experiences in the real world had no influence on how the Firm does things, her views had little impact on the royal family, and her unhappiness and her struggles were not that important to her husband.

In the accompanying figure is the Competing Values Framework with a selection of popular songs that illustrate each model.

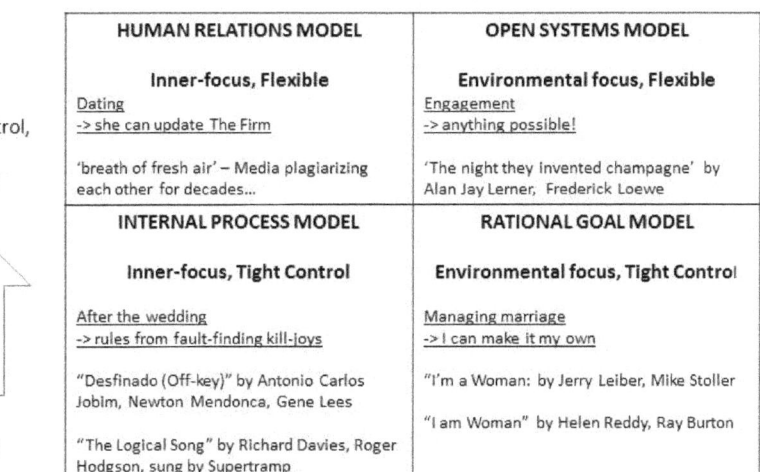

i. HR Fail: Talent walks out the door

Nowadays a newcomer told to sink-or-swim is more likely to drown or is more likely to flame out from the pressure and unfamiliarity with the culture. Raising the bar higher and higher, public life had never been 24/7 as it is today – moreover, in the old days, everyone was more deferential (Merrick, 2018). Sarah Ferguson, Duchess of York, reports palace courtiers, the Grey Men of the establishment, treated newcomers like her shortcomings with hostility and impatience. This negative feedback mistakenly was thought to motivate; rather, it pushes her away. Love <u>Won't</u> Keep Us Together if the newly minted princess gets insufficient orientation and training and support for her role.

Sometimes she fades and loses her personality; sometimes she flames out. The problems faced by Michiko Shoda when she married into the Japanese imperial family are so well known that eligible Japanese women hurriedly did whatever they possible to get kicked off the shortlist for her son, Crown Prince Naruhito. If that meant getting on a one-way ticket out of the land of the rising sun, getting married or getting their ears pierced, so be it (Klein, 1993).

> "The problem is that she's got to remember that, as a member of the royal family, she represents the family or, as it's been called, 'the brand'," said Grant Harrold, who served as a butler to Harry himself while working for his father Prince Charles, and now provides expert guidance on the subject.

> "So, I think there is quite a lot pressure to make sure she gets it right because the last thing she wants to do is do something wrong or make a mistake and it ends up becoming front page news - and then it's embarrassing for her and for the royal family," **(Mills, 2018)**

Amanda Horne's examples of incivility must be familiar to royal newcomers from Lady Diana Spencer, Sarah Ferguson to Michiko Shoda: "glaring, rolling eyes and other unpleasant expressions, teasing, putting people down, treating people like they're invisible, back stabbing, micromanaging, insulting, belittling, deflating, disrespecting, de-energizing, rudely interrupting, being mean-spirited, nasty, and tyrannical." (Home, 2009)

Robert I Sutton, professor of management science and engineering at Stanford University and author of *The No-Assholes Rule: Building a Civilized Workplace and Surviving One That Isn't*, advises that organizations need to both "screen for jerks as they hire and purge the bullies already in the ranks because, in almost all cases, they cost more than they contribute," (Associated Press, 2007). He also says that for anyone with less power, the best solution is to quit. Less ideal is to either minimize contact with the jerks or checking out emotionally.

The many issues of poor training include organizational stress, marital stress, and work not getting done, as the stressed princess does not meet often unrealistic performance expectations. As William James had concluded, poor self-esteem results when the set of expectations and the record of achievement do not match.

She may end up with such contempt for a poorly-managed, abusive organization that the new princess retaliates with covert activities, prepares to jump ship, or undermines the firm through sabotage. If she comes to the conclusion that her efforts and sacrifices are unappreciated and likely to remain so, she can act out.

> "Problems begin to arise when they confuse their private and their public lives and start to think that the public is interested in them for who they really are, rather than what they represent. Then things go really haywire when they go off-script and start to perform the lead role in their own psychodramas." (Brown C., 2018)

The discouraged princess may react through negligence of duty and behavior, become a hedonistic glutton for the shallow luxuries, feel entitled, nag, act irresponsibly, focus on getting Botox, dieting and hanging out with different versions of the spoiled Park Avenue Princess. In short, she may end up rebelling against a toxic work environment and abusive management and colleagues - like 78% of people do when confronted by incivility.

And then she might take Professor Sutton's advice and call it quits. Talent walks out the door.

ii. The Firm's dilemma: Shift or Go Extinct

Since the very public divorces of Diana, Sarah, and former Princess Alexandra of Denmark, there is a recognition across the royal house world of the need to adopt a pro-active HRM strategy. Some taxpayers balk at footing the security costs of royal weddings and protest through petitions (Embury-Dennis, 2018), with The Rt Rev Pete Broadbent, the Bishop of Willesden, going public on Facebook (Ward, 2010), which he later apologized for and was suspended from his post, disillusioned with funding a procession of marriages that do not make it past a dozen years of public happiness. Perhaps it is this sentiment that is at the roots of a YouGov poll on the nuptials of Prince Harry and Meghan Markle. In contrast to the media hype, the wedding is not turning on a majority of the responders to the poll (Lusher, Huge drop in number of royal wedding street parties compared to Will and Kate's big day, 2018). Craig Brown reports on veteran royal watchers taking bets on how long Prince Harry and Meghan Markle's marriage would last (Brown C. , 2018)

Contrast the four steps of HR-lite with the nine HRM practices of a top-performing firm:

1. Needs identification
2. Job Design
3. Job Posting
4. Candidate review
5. Interviewing
6. Hiring
7. Training & Orientation (and coaching)
8. Performance Review (and Discipline)
9. Exit Interview/Promotion

It is evident that this model emphasizes proactivity. It does not wait, it anticipates (Needs Identification), and shapes hiring by updating the posting (job design), adding a full training and coaching element, and as such plays a major role in the firm's strategic orientation.

In a March 2009 interview to promote *Young Victoria*, a film she co-produced, Sarah, Duchess of York, spoke about lack of orientation and other shortcomings of the HRM in the British Monarchy:

> "'You have to think of the Royal family as being like a brand, yah? There are CEOs protecting the brand, and I didn't really fit in. Maybe if I'd had an adviser to lead me through it all I would have weathered it a bit better. I wish I had done it differently. I wish I could do it all over again." (Cavendish, 2009)

Anyone needing further convincing of the efficacy and success of a more involved HRM policy should look at the success of the reality show world. On *So You Think You can Dance*, *Strictly Come Dancing*, *The Apprentice*, and *American Idol*, the audition process takes the best of a select pool of worthy candidates. As Nigel Lythgoe says, they want to gets people before a large audience weekly to test how they can learn, get along, and exhibit stamina to be crowned America's favourite dancer.

Both the new employee and the organization benefit from an intensive and extensive training period. With a coach who can counsel and listen, the newbie princess develops a collaborative relationship with the firm. In gratitude that the firm demonstrates its support for her, she buys into it – this is diversity and inclusion in action (Nordell, 2018). She is thus better acculturated into the firm and more likely to succeed, as in Mary Donaldson, who married Crown Prince Frederik of Denmark (Jane, 2018).

A more intensive vetting and training period in what matters most for the job. The media gushing influences that slightly; but more significant are internal rivalries and failure to conduct a needs-analysis and allocate enough funding to train and develop – media and marketing.

> "Bolland explains that the royal family's 'do nothing, say nothing' policy is utterly wrongheaded. '…you can't pursue a policy that regards the media as the enemy'. Bolland's policy was radically different… He steered Prince Charles towards media-friendly photocalls…, regularly briefed the press with stories that showed the prince in a good light… He made his

crotchety, insecure, old-fashioned and out-of-touch boss seem human." (Byrnes, 2005)

Driving systemic change internally by the executives of the Firm is to proactively keep its fingers on the pulse of the nation, to survive by shifting as things shift. It is in the Firm's best interest to get out of inertia (Sykes, Meghan Markle Can Help the Royal Family Change—If It Wants To, 2018), stop resisting change - or it is forced by the populace to change. Which is what happened to the ruling house of Nepal.

Nepal is the latest country that swiftly removed what its people perceived as an insensitive and unresponsive monarchy. Rather than bringing out the best in its people and capitalizing on the sympathy brought about in 2003 when the crown prince went on a shooting rampage and assassinated his immediate family, the new king reverted to absolute rule, suspending representative democracy. After three years of violent protests, the king relented. By then, it was too late - the fractious political parties united to force a drastic change, which was to abolish the monarchy entirely (Sharma, 2008).

Graham Smith of the anti-monarchist group, Republicans, has gone on record: "The royals are running out of fresh ideas and big PR opportunities – now the real debate about this rotten institution must begin. We're not a nation of republicans yet – but we've stopped being a nation of royalists." (Lusher, Huge drop in number of royal wedding street parties compared to Will and Kate's big day, 2018)

Bhutan, on the other hand, has managed to survive by making way - its royal family decided that King Jigme Singye would abdicate in favour of his heir. There is a balance between respecting the institutional memory of experienced courtiers and taking on professionals who respond to a changing environment. A new young sovereign to usher in change and openness, King Jigme Khesar Namgyel is the appealing front man of the new Cool Bhutan, democratic, respectful of its cultural heritage and environment, and open to tourism. His queen Jetsun Pema happens to be intelligent, and their new son looks like a cherub.

3. She's got Personality

In the study of human behavior, certain ways of behaving are consistent for certain groups of people, and taken together is these make up personality. Personality is an integral part of an individual's psychological makeup – this pattern of behavior can be extremely appealing to others as per Lloyd Price's hit song, Personality (Price & Logan, 2014). The two most common instruments to categorize personality used by researchers and human resources specialists are the Big Five (CANOE: conscientiousness, agreeableness, neuroticisim, openness, extroversion) and the Myers-Briggs Type Indicator (MBTI). These focus on an individual's actions (behaviours), the Enneagram looks at the motivations that drive the behaviours.

What the HRM model focuses on is adapting the new hire to the culture of the organization. It lacks attention to one key step – accounting for personality type. Each personality has a unique strategy in life and by understanding what this is, the organization and the individual can collaborate to meet the goals of the firm and of the new hire.

In recent years, the Enneagram has become a professional development tool used by industrial /organizational consultants working with firms such as the Central Intelligence Agency (CIA), Pacific Gas and Electricity Company (PG&E), and Hewlett Packard (Tilsner, 1995). It is most commonly employed for the purposes of enhancing sales and productivity.

Clients and their needs are the focus of many Enneagram presentations in business. Organizations expect that learning about people through the Enneagram enables their staff to better understand clients and provide enhanced customer service. Judy George, CEO and founder of Boston-based Domain Home Fashions (Summers, 1999) has adapted the Enneagram in the design of a customer self-assessment instrument in an effort to drive sales. Morris and Cramer (1996) suggest that libraries could function more effectively when staff receive training in the Enneagram. Frontline workers can also work together more efficiently when they anticipate how various Enneagram personality types make use of the library.

The Enneagram personality system working within HRM has been influential in many organizations – including major corporations and the CIA - and it offers monarchies a way forward. There are nine life strategies with predictable patterns of behavior when someone is at his or her normal self, the home space. Oftentimes, it is remarkable how differently someone reacts under difficult circumstances in a manner that is at odds with what is normal for him or her. The Enneagram system accounts for this set of behaviours under stress (compulsion) and another set under total relaxation (deliberate choice), according to Enneagram teacher Sister Patricia Shreenan (Sister Patricia Shreenan, 2018).

Understanding the Enneagram will further expand the HRM success of royal Firms everywhere, especially in the recruitment and training area. Moreover, it prompts an alignment of the issues of concern of the individual with those of the Firm. By engaging on a personal level with the individual, the organization initiates from a health-promotion perspective that spreads throughout the team and ultimately acculturates the entire staff. It is thus by appreciating and honouring the strengths of each individual team member that ironically the institution moves forward as an entity.

This book series focuses on the applications of the Enneagram as it relates to HRM of non-royal women to the ranks of reigning royalty. In so doing there will only the occasional spotlight on the cases of royals marrying royals (Duchess Sophie in Bavaria to crown Prince Alois von Liechtenstein) and marriages to non-reigning royals (Clotilde Coureau to the Prince of Venice and Diana de Cadaval to Prince Charles Phillippe d'Orléans of France, Maria Margarita de Vargas y Santaella to Luis Alfonso de Borbon).

A. *The Enneagram Personality System*

Based on my own research into the Enneagram and organizational health promotion and years as a royal watcher, I have been analyzing how applying HRM strategies work with the 9 personality styles. A large part of the usefulness of the Enneagram is how these 9 discrete personalities are intricately related.

This will enable you to understand the life strategy of your favourite royal princess in her home space, and how that personality style sees people and the external world.

When anyone is properly valued and honoured for being Who They Are, they are in that state of ultimate relaxation and receptivity, expanding and stretching their own home space capacity of behavioural patterns to go beyond this comfort zone. We all know people who release themselves into behaviours, actions, and attitudes previously unseen by the outside world under conditions of utter joy. Research into the theories behind Accelerated Learning, much of it attributed the Bulgarian scientist, George Lozanov, offers that learning widens and deepens in relaxation. In effect, the mind becomes more open and receptive to both long-term and short-term learning and retention. (Rose & Nicholl, 1996)

Under conditions of stress from any combination of negative feedback, lack of support, and underappreciation, on the contrary, leads to internal shut down. The individual retreats into self and in a sense regresses in behavior. Retreating into negativity versions of home space, a royal princess becomes BitterGirl. Prolonged time spent in this unhealthy state brings out the worst of herself, a rage that spreads outwardly, resulting in behaviours that convey the message of self-loathing.

The Enneagram thus has the potential as a useful guide to the warning signs when someone is regressing in compulsion into Her Worst Self. It offers strategies to respond to it and as a tool of health promotion ways to enhance the Better Self of the 9 personality styles.

This book aims to point out typical Enneagram personality styles, via analysis of her interviews, interactions, and media portrayals of new princesses.

i. Overview

This overview is adapted from my dissertation - more about the Enneagram, please see the references provided at the end of the book.

The Enneagram (from the Greek words: *ennea* "nine" +*gram* "something drawn") is at its simplest form, a nine-point star figure comprised of a circle in which is contained an equilateral triangle sitting on its base and touching the edges of the circle at its points (Palmer & Brown, 1997). It has been used as a theory of personality, a process of personal development, a guide to interpersonal relationships, and many other personal development domains. The roots of Enneagram thinking, although not clear, appear to be early Christian or Sufi.

Passed on by oral tradition from its beginnings, the Enneagram was first known to the West in the early 20th century via the work of George Ivanovich Gurdjieff, who conducted research on mystical traditions of various religions. Oscar Ichazo, teaching in Bolivia and Chile, became familiar with Gurdjieff and saw the applications of the Enneagram to the study of personality. Refining the Enneagram's psychological aspects was American psychiatrist Claudio Naranjo from the Esalen Institute in California, who introduced the Enneagram theory in the United States (Rohr & Ebert, 2001). Beginning in the 1970s, the Enneagram, which had hitherto been orally transmitted, became more widely known as various Enneagram students began writing about their experiences (Colina, 1996) – that the Enneagram is a psychological and spiritual map delineating the realm of ego (Maitri, 2000).

Since the last quarter of the 20th century, the Enneagram had been largely written about in terms of individual development and personality. Books, magazine articles, and journal articles have focused principally on the Enneagram's applications in psychology, religion, business, and the development of Enneagram personality typing instruments. There are reports of ongoing experimental research into the Enneagram as a psychological tool, although to date limited research has been published in academic journals.

Writers and researchers of the Enneagram offer differing interpretations of the theory , some focusing on levels of psychological development with a vocabulary that includes wings and arrows, such as Riso & Hudson (2000) and others on intuition, shifting attention and awareness such as Palmer (1988) which are beyond the scope of this overview. However, they all agree on the basics of the Enneagram, that the triangle represents the three centres of the individual. They see the Enneagram as a model of intrapersonal dynamics in which the self is comprised of three centres of knowing - Intellectual, Relational, and Creative (Figure 2). Each centre has a different orientation – Intellectual towards facts and logic, Relational towards feelings and people, and Creative towards doing and instincts.

The Three Enneagram Centers of Self

Purpose & Functioning of Centre	Terminology According to Enneagram Author		
	Hurley & Donsson	Palmer & Daniels, Rohr & Ebert, Goldberg	Riso & Hudson
Movement, Intent, Enactment (Doing)	Creative	Gut	Instinctual
Connectedness, Relatedness, Transcendance (Feeling)	Relational	Heart	Feeling
Vision, Awareness, True Meaning of Reality (Thinking)	Intellectual	Head	Thinking

Sources: Hurley, K & Dobson, T. (1993). *My Best Self: Using the Enneagram to Free the Soul*. New York City: HarperCollins Publishers. Goldberg, M. J., (1999). Nine ways of working: How to Use the Enneagram to Discover Your Natural Strengths and Work More Effectively. Marlowe & Co.: New York. Palmer, H. & Brown, P. B. (1997). The Enneagram Advantage: Putting the Nine Personality Types to Work in the Office. New York: Three Rivers Press. Riso, D. R. & Hudson, R. (1999). The Wisdom of the Enneagram: The Complete Guide to Psychological and Spiritual Growth for the Nine Personality Types. Bantam Books: New York. Rohr, R. & Ebert, A. (2001). The Enneagram: A Christian Perspective. The Crossroad Publishing Company: New York.

ROYALTY MEETS ENNEAGRAM: UNDERSTANDING PERSONALITY STYLE 7

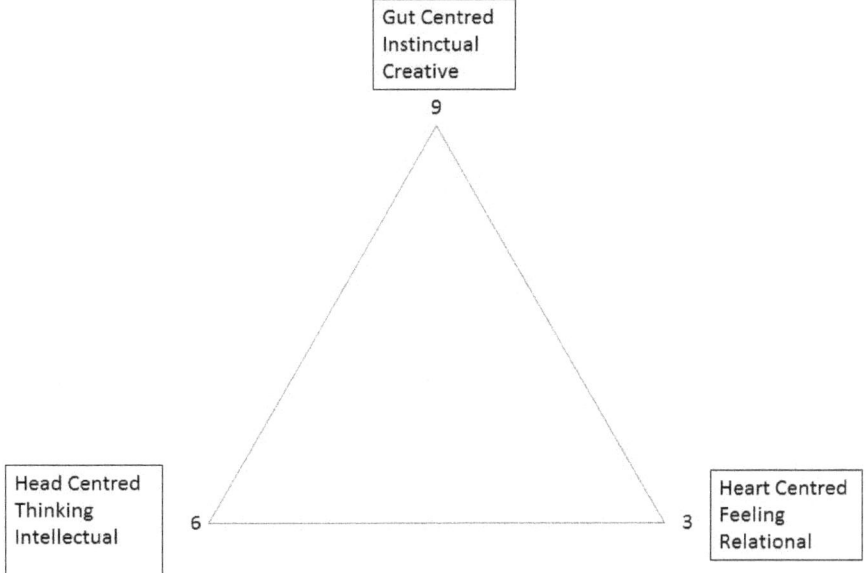

Three Centres of Self: Terminology Used by Enneagram writers

In a healthy individual, the three centres of self are of equal value. Kathy Hurley and Theodorre Donson hypothesize that individuals early on in life move away from valuing and functioning within each of these centres equally. The person focuses on one centre over the other two - as that centre provides an effective survival strategy. In a family where logical discourse, suppressed emotions, and planning are modelled, an individual may adopt the strategy of the Intellectual Center. Over time, this becomes the dominant habitual survival strategy. "We cling too much to what comes our way naturally…" (Rohr & Ebert, 2001, p. 12).

A person can approach his or her dominant centre in one of three orientations: outer-directed (external environment), inner-directed (inner world), or harmonizing (balancing the external environment and interior self). From each centre emerge three personalities – totalling nine Enneagram personalities as illustrated by the previous figure (Hurley & Dobson, 1993). The accompanying figure illustrates how these personalities fit on the Enneagram itself, in bold are my descriptors of the princess's personality.

Preferred Center	Orientation Towards Use of Preferred Center		
	Outer directed	Inner directed	Harmonizers
Gut CREATIVE (Doing)	8 Take charge Boedica	1 Rules & Standards Enforcer	9 Common Ground Consensus Builder
Heart RELATIONAL (Feeling)	2 Helping Compassionate Helper	4 Honoring uniqueness Unforgettable	3 Goals & Targets Worker Bee
Head INTELLECTUAL (Thinking)	7 Making a splash The Promoter	5 Analysing Investigator	6 Guarding the castle Loyal Defender

Author's sources include Hurley, K & Dobson, T. (1993). *My Best Self: Using the Enneagram to Free the Soul*. New York City: HarperCollins Publishers.

Unfortunately, after many years, one orientation in the dominant center unwittingly is seen as the sole successful life strategy, and eventually this becomes habitual: "perceives 360 degrees of reality in a very limited way and most of our decisions and interests are found on highly sophisticated habits, rather than freedom of choice." (Palmer, 1988, p. 21) In the long run, the individual depends on the strategies of that centre almost exclusively, to the detriment of healthy personal growth and development: "We are destroyed by our gifts because we identify too closely with what we can do well." (Rohr & Ebert, 2001, p. 23). One centre is overemphasized as an effective life strategy, the other two are neglected. In daily life, this neglect could be in the form of misuse or disuse. The solution to unhealthy states, according to Hurley and Donsson (1999), is to re-evaluate one's fundamental assumptions, discover how the centres became off-balance, and work towards rebalancing.

ii. Royalty meets Enneagram

This book takes Enneagram application a step forward by examining the nine types of royal princess roles, giving modern examples of how new princesses's performance meet The Firm's goal of survival.

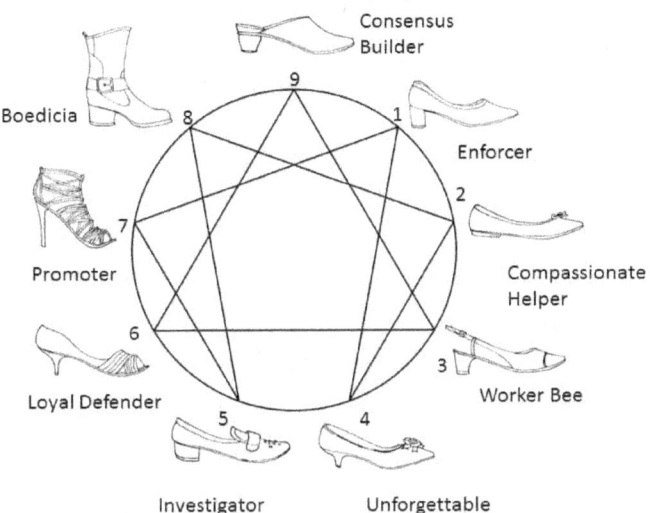

Success in an organization depends on the degree of receptivity to the newcomer's ideas (flexibility) in the overall culture and a strong training and mentorship of individuals that is tailored to their personality. They should be coached in how to manage the stress of carrying out their duties, how to pace themselves, learning to set boundaries. The Enneagram gives clues on a type's intrinsic motivation.

The organization itself should not feel envious when the pupil succeeds, as success preserves the organization, and those who get jealous should be reminded to focus on the bigger picture. That is where mentors come in, to address the internal conflict amongst the

Old Guard and to value in the newcomer's growing awareness and helping communicate her insights to the rest of the court. Gradual socialization into the organization enables the new princess to learn the written and unspoken rules of the organization's culture.

Moving from the individual level to the group level, she will build alliances to further refine the culture. In this new stage of the organization - which comes about only after an extended period of initiation and time in boot camp and proving your worth which some have chafed at ie Sarah Ferguson – then she is given room to participate in team formation and decisions.

Jockeying for position, power, negotiating, and influencing the power brokers means looking for as much face time as possible. In the UK, even the British Prime Minister does not take lightly the Queen's summer break at Balmoral. Diana suffered her morning rides with the Queen, not seeing it as a perk but as a punishment. That's precious face time with the boss! Similarly, the stresses that come with interpersonal interactions can be predicted and managed via the Enneagram.

> "Men and women… tend to experience work outside the home in different ways…. Full-time, professional women with families might have lower self-esteem not because they are accomplishing less, but because they expect more from themselves than they can possibly deliver." (Csikszentmihalyi, 1998)

At the point where she can be trusted to do the front-line work without active supervision, as someone has a comfortable grasp of the inner processes, paying your dues, mastering the rules, serving time as a probationary employee, showing understanding of your place in the scheme of things (Foster, 2018), only then can the new princess be taken seriously as a member of the Inner Cabinet of the Firm's board of directors. In the UK, the core of the royal family were reputed to have formed a Way Forward steering committee (Williams, 1998), perhaps discussing visioning, goal-setting, strategy, human resources recruitment, and organizational and job design. In Competing Values Framework I would say she needs to master the inner workings first. That way she earns her way to the Human Relations model and can contribute to making a difference. Change the world comes after putting in the time.

B. Princess Enneagram Personality Type by Shoe Styles

If the new princess dons shoes that correspond solely to her personality type, I offer the following way to remember her Enneagram style:

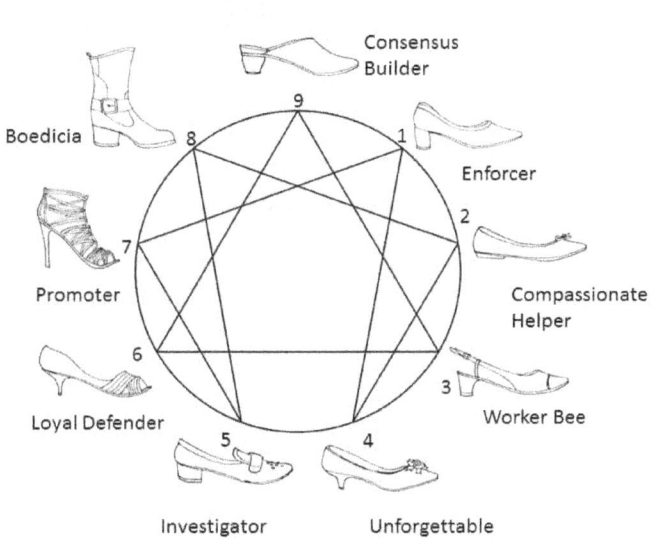

\# 1 – Rules & Standards – The Enforcer wears medium heeled court shoes. Her heels are grounded in codes and tradition

2 – Helping Others – The Compassionate Helper needs practical footwear for getting close to the children like the classic Ballerina shoes from Repetto http://www.repetto.com/en/women/women-shoes/ballerinas.html

3 – Hitting goals & targets – The Worker Bee combines style and comfort by donning Slingbacks

4 – Honoring uniqueness – She's Unforgettable and so are her kitten heels with appliques

5 – Analyzing – The Investigator's footwear is seriously Oxford

6 – Guarding the castle – The Loyal Defender scans to see who has her back and can risk wearing peep-toe shoes

7 – Make an Entrance and a splash – The Promoter gets all eyes upon entering any room in Gladiators with stiletto heels

8 – Take Charge – Boedicia has the boots that are made for walkin'

9 – Finding Common Ground – The Consensus builder is as comfortable and ubiquitous as her slip-on mules

4. Enneagram 7: The Promoter

Three women and their lives and choices illustrate the Enneagram 7 Promoter personality quite closely: Tessy Antony de Nassau, Princess of Luxembourg (32), Meghan Markle (36) actress from California, Sarah Ferguson Duchess of York (58) from British gentry.

The moment she came into the public eye vis-à-vis her royal beau, the descriptors included energetic, optimistic. "A breath of fresh air" is a term often used to describe the potential impact of an Enneagram 7 Promoter personality, as was for Sarah Ferguson (Sales, 2011). She does not come alone, often she is surrounded by like-minded people, they are an entourage of positive thinking and living. They do it with verve! Enneagram author Karen Webb says Enneagram 7s are natural networkers, who easily make connections, a gift that keeps on giving in social situations. Everyone likes her natural ease with people and adapting to different environments. She likes to meet people and learn new experiences, presents a cheerful persona.

Its chorus sung by generations of Scouts, *Keep on the Sunny Side*, by Ada Blenkhorn and Howard Entwisle might as well be the anthem of the Enneagram 7 Promoter Princess (The CyberHymnal, 2017):

> Stay on the sunny side,
> Always on the sunny side,
> Stay on the sunny side of life.
> You'll feel no pain as we drive you insane,
> If you'll stay on the sunny side of life.
> (Boy Scout Trail, 2018)

<u>Sister Patricia Shreenan</u>, the Victoria-based Canadian of the sisters of St Ann (SSA) teaches the Enneagram personality system from the Narrative Tradition perspective. Trained with <u>Helen Palmer</u> and <u>David Daniels</u>, she states, "Where Attention flows, Energy goes." (Shreenan, 2011) Sister Patricia is of the opinion that the most effective mentoring is "pioneering processes of 'individualized learning'. If someone is compulsively going about life at the mercy of his or her habitual behaviours, then in effect 'you are at your wit's end'. Only by increasing self awareness of what motivates your core can you take deliberate action in life.

Energy goes toward creating actions based on attention that certain needs have to be met. For the Enneagram 7 Promoter Princess, these actions are to promote the positive, seek out options, foster innovation, keep an eye on a bright future. In the Competing Values Framework, she is naturally most at ease in the Open Systems quadrant —with no rules, the world is your oyster.

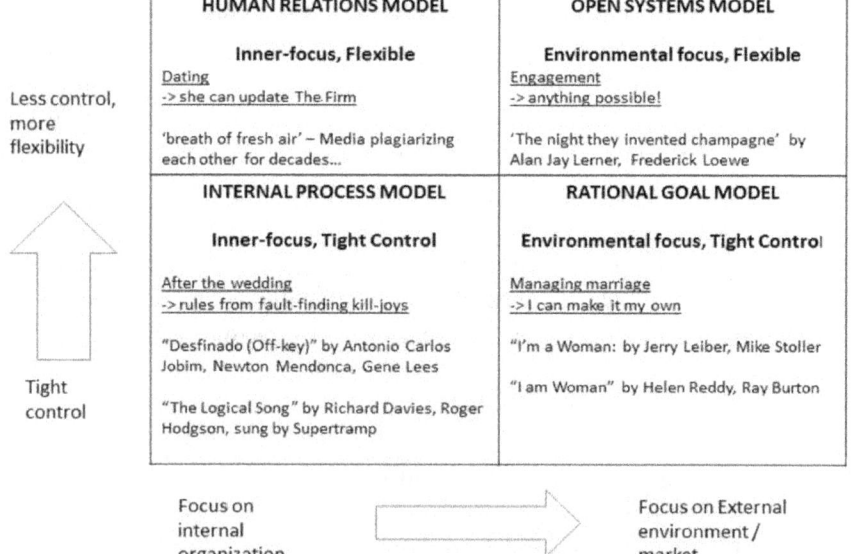

If life is an amusement park, she must try everything. This is rooted in the 3 Fs: FOMO , fear of missing out (Hobson, 2018); FOBLO, fear of being left out; and FOGKO, fear of getting kicked out, the latter coined by Professor Deborah Tannen (Kiefer, 2017). At the inner core of the Enneagram 7 Promoter Princess's life strategy, the intention of seeing everything, is an underlying anxiety about the negative shadowy side of life. By focusing on optimism and keeping an eye out for imminent positive experiences, she can keep negativity and the 3 Fs (FOMO, FOBLO, FOGKO) at bay.

Notice the life strategy of avoiding painful emotions by valiantly focusing only on the upbeat and positive in this statement by Sarah Ferguson:

> The selection of Sarah, Duchess of York ("Fergie"), as
> a UN goodwill ambassador with special responsibility for refugees was made amid considerable fanfare in 1993.... Not only did she have a good reputation for civic engagement from her work as the founder and life president of the UK charity Children in Crisis, but she had a flair and vigor that were very attractive. At the announcement of her appointment, Fergie stated: "I'm not just going to be a letterhead. I am
> very, very serious about it. I want to do much more to help. I am good at talking about things. (Cooper, 2007)

The motivation for the forward-fun-future orientation is to avoid pain. In fact, the Enneagram 7 Promoter Princess's attitude towards pain is not at all favourable. Now the obvious reaction to this statement is: who in heaven's name is actually in favour of pain?

No one actually likes pain but most will concede that there is a benefit to pain. If you do not feel pain when you do a face-plant, fail your driver's licence road test, hurt from unrequited love, weep at a family funeral, you would not learn from your mistakes nor would you grasp the fullness of the human experience. The attitude of most people is that pain is unwelcome, but an inevitable part of living.

"That's what YOU think!" would be the response from the Enneagram 7 Promoter Princess. Their unconscious attitude is instead that pain is debilitating and of no benefit whatsoever. The Promoter avoids as much as possible the emotional pain of being shunned and the outsider status of the 3 Fs (FOMO, FOBLO, FOGKO).

Meghan Markle has seen how fleeting fortune can be – according to her older half-brother Thomas Markle Jr, among other grievances, their father had won a lottery prize of more than half a million US dollars when she was 9 and living full time with her divorced mother. A good father, he used some of that money for Meghan to attend private school and private Northwestern University in Chicago (Andrews, 2018). She acknowledges this in interviews.

Of those who think pain is inevitable, the Promoter's opinion is that they have simply given into this fatalistic attitude or they have not done enough to keep pain out of their lives. Truth be told, the Promoter is correct in that some pain can be avoided if you do whatever it takes to keep well away from danger, risky activities, and people who are pain-magnets. Don't give into the gloominess of today! Don't give up, look at the wonderful possibilities for a brighter future!

A. Her Strengths

Newcomers in town, if you want to see the highlights, go with an Enneagram 7 Promoter Princess! She either can give you a good tour or have enough people to provide you with the best of the city. She has lots of energy – unlike Jeb Bush who was slighted by Donald Trump for his 'low energy' (Parker, 2015)

When life were Christmas meal, she would serve it as a buffet. Think of a Las Vegas buffet with a huge variety available 24/7. The place never closes. And she's always ready for action.

i. All over the World

Many experiences in life and many places to experience is what the Enneagram 7 Promoter princess thinks of globalization, and the theme song is from the Electric Light Orchestra (ELO) *All Over the World* https://www.youtube.com/watch?v=X3N9SVfs0jg .

Princess Tessy currently works for Vice Impact as director of EMEA, Europe, Middle East, and Asia, a portfolio that leaves out very few parts of the world. What seemed to have started it all was signing up at age 18 for the rigor of the Luxembourg Army and later deployment to Kosovo as part of a UN Peacekeeping force and stints in the Luxembourg embassies in Geneva and London. She is the first in her family to obtain a degree, studying at universities outside of Luxembourg as her marriage and motherhood took her to living and studying in Florida, then London. Travels to Africa were part of her efforts with UN-AIDS and other charitable organizations.

In a June 2013 interview with Marie Clarie, Meghan Markle mentions her love of travel:

> "I love to travel, too. My most recent trips in the past year-and-a-half have been biking through Vietnam, campervanning through New Zealand, and touring the whole coast of Croatia and the islands there. I always want off-the-beaten-path, Anthony Bourdain–inspired travel." (Brannigan, 2018)

After high school, Meghan made the most of her college years by leaving the sunshine of SoCal to study in Chicago's Northwestern University. Chicago is called The Windy City for a reason. It gets blustery cold in winter too! A self-described theater nerd, she also pledged into a sorority club (Samuelson, 2017). The study abroad options offered by Northwestern speak very much to their Open Systems Model ethos as per the Competing Values Framework. As Promoter, Meghan's own outlook aligned very well with the university's mission. With the assistance of her diplomat uncle, Michael Markle, she spent a few months on internship at the US embassy in Buenos Aires. Later, she spent some of her third year in Madrid.

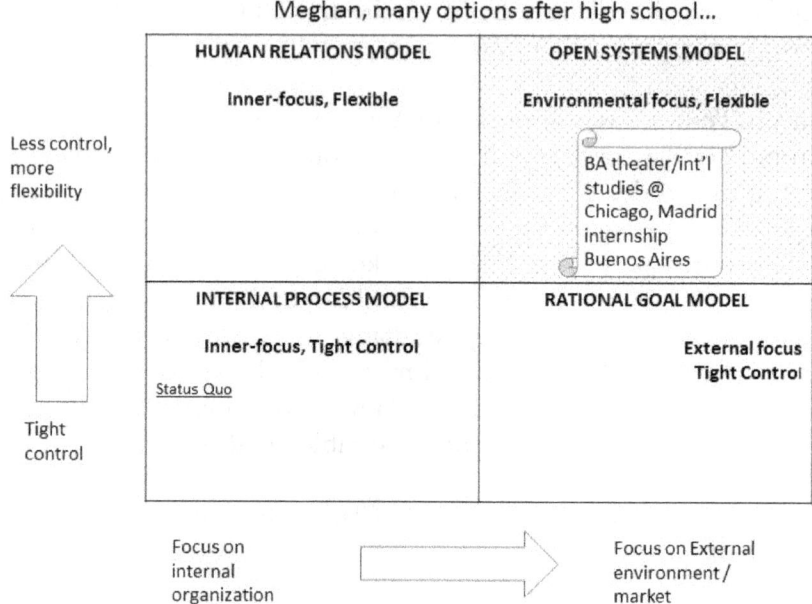

Sarah Ferguson wrote in her biography, *My Life*, about backpacking with a chum from Argentina, South America to the US. In 2011, she filmed 'Finding Sarah: *From Royalty to the Real World*' (Oprah Winfrey Network, 2011) an Oprah Winfrey Network six-part mini-series that was an adventure travelogue from the UK to the US and even Yellowknife, in Canada's Arctic.

Sarah Ferguson wrote and edited books on a variety of topics before and during marriage. Afterwards, she published books that put herself front and centre on the cover - *Travels with Queen Victoria* and diet and self-esteem books *Finding Sarah*. And on the film *Young Victoria*, she was a producer. Her work is a little bit of this and a little bit of that. Extremely creative, the Enneagram 7 Promoter princess lives in the future where art of the possible is always possible. Pushing beyond your comfort zone is something the Seven does to drink deeply out of the Cup of Life. When the scholastic environment fosters that, then things like advocacy happen.

For example, for Sarah Ferguson, it is starting her own charity. For Meghan Markle, it was through the auspices of The Immaculate Heart High School and Middle School, the girls-only private school in Los Feliz, Los Angeles where she studied. Going beyond the privileged enclave to be among 'the poor, the marginalized, the voiceless, the underserved' is expected of all students as per the Community Service page of the school website (Immaculate Heart High School & Middle School, 2018) . The president of Immaculate Heart puts Meghan Markle's charity work in the context of other alumnae:

> "Over 10,000 women of great heart and right conscience have graduated from Immaculate Heart – and we are proud to count Meghan Markle, Class of 1999, among that number," said Maureen Diekmann, president of Immaculate Heart." (Park LaBrea News Beverly Press, 2017)

ii. We're here for a good time, not a long time…

The 1977 hit song by Canadian group, Trooper, 'We're here for a good time, not a long time" by Ra McGuire & Brian Smith (Trooper, 2018) https://www.youtube.com/watch?v=8gCjJC_INNE point out how important a positive outlook is for the Enneagram 7. Bright-eye and bushy-tailed, it is no wonder that Sarah Ferguson, Meghan Markle, and Princess Tessy seem natural in front of the camera.

They really are genuinely happy to be there in front of an audience.

When Sarah was married to Andrew, the Duchess of York always gave it her all in public appearances, usually doing something memorable and for a while brought back into fashion hair bows (Rodger, 2017) and hair snoods (Iverem, 1988). Sarah Ferguson is upbeat in her media and television appearances, even taking the chair for CNN's Larry King on a few occasions. It takes chutzpah for Sarah to write a cookbook and airily confess on television that she can't cook (BBC, 1998)

Princess Tessy invited a television crew to follow her around in the aftermath of her divorce, talking about her professional work and her charity work. (RTL.lu, 2017) Choosing jewelry and clothes to bring a touch of glamour, to bring her A-game to a charity function, she is candid about living as a single working parent in London. The joy of Enneagram 7 Promoter Princess, however, is also discovering and promoting new talent.. Tessy can give little-known designers for example like those featured at Little Black Dress a platform to show off their feminine and gorgeous designs to the media (Little Black Dress, 2017).

Meghan Markle similarly had shared glimpses of her home, glamourous entertainment industry lifestyle, and preferred products on her lifestyle blog 'The Tig', named after a fine Italian wine, on various social media accounts. She makes no bones about striving for acting parts, as she calls it 'hustling' (Hardy, 2017) and that the successful outcome of being driven to overcome obstacles and continuing to audition is this fabulous lifestyle.

After her engagement, she continues to champion little-known Canadian fashion and accessory brand designers, especially those in her closet from her Toronto filming days with *Suits* (Deschamps, 2018). Patronizing certain fashion labels as a style influencer, she has worn Birks, Reitmans, Aritizia, and other stylish fashions from The Great White North. (O'Connor, 2018)

> "…she seems to thrive on being in the royal limelight. Her extraordinary self-confidence has taken some of Harry's circle by surprise, so different is she from anyone else he has dated. At the same time, they feel her composure is probably what he has been subconsciously seeking for years. (Kay & Levy, Why 'nice but clingy' Harry is marrying Meghan - and not any of his MANY former flames: Prince's complex psychology revealed by Britain's top royal writers, 2018)

Anyone who has something to promote knows you have to court publicity. Shying away from the cameras and not giving the media something positive and optimistic to write about does not serve the cause.

iii. Fun fun fun

There is being positive and optimistic and then there is cutting loose – the Enneagram 7 Promoter princess throws herself body and soul into making life uber-fun. The hit by The Beach Boys says it all, Fun fun fun

Sarah Ferguson is extremely sporty outdoors with downhill skiing and as a longtime horsewoman (Jordan, 2009) Because Andrew trained as a pilot, Sarah wanted to share his love of the skies. She learnt to fly a plane and pilot a helicopter, the Piper Warrior and Jet Ranger, which involve high energy and risk taking (Burke, 2009). Note that she never got seriously interested in Andrew's other love, golf, which requires precision, patience, and silence.

Take the traditional wedding and shake out the conventional, that is how the Enneagram 7 Promoter Princess puts her personal lighthearted stamp on the event. Sarah Ferguson reverted to the older Anglican wedding service of promising to 'obey' her husband, Prince Andrew (Wallace, 1986). A tongue-in-cheek move, as if anyone believed Sarah meekly following Andrew's dictates!

Some couples who have lived together for years choose a discreet registry office to get married in like Carrie Bradshaw and John Preston (Sex and The City movie) but it was not the case for Meghan Markle and Trevor Engelson who went all out for a four-day destination wedding in September 2011. They eschewed the church and synagogue in favour of four-day Caribbean beach celebration with friends and family at the Jamaica Inn luxury resort, Ochos Rios. (Duncan, 2018)

Meghan may be seen by some as 'mothering' Prince Harry but she makes sure they both have fun in her so doing (Maxtone Graham, 2018). Her second wedding was even bigger than her first! Their wedding service includes the modern pop hit *Stand by Me* and the spiritual *This Little Light of Mine*. (Stickings & English, 2018)

When Tessy became a mother at age 20, as an Enneagram 7, the army corporal moved from an Open Systems Model to the Human Relations model, focused and disciplined in her approach to parenting and being a spouse and a student. But still… a fun mum! After the 2006 civil wedding to Prince Louis in the Grand Ducal palace, Tessy Antony went to the religious wedding in a picturesque church in Gilsdorf, Luxembourg accompanied by their adorable 6-month old son, Gabriel de Nassau, while wearing a eye-catching strapless white wedding gown. (Order of Splendour, 2011).

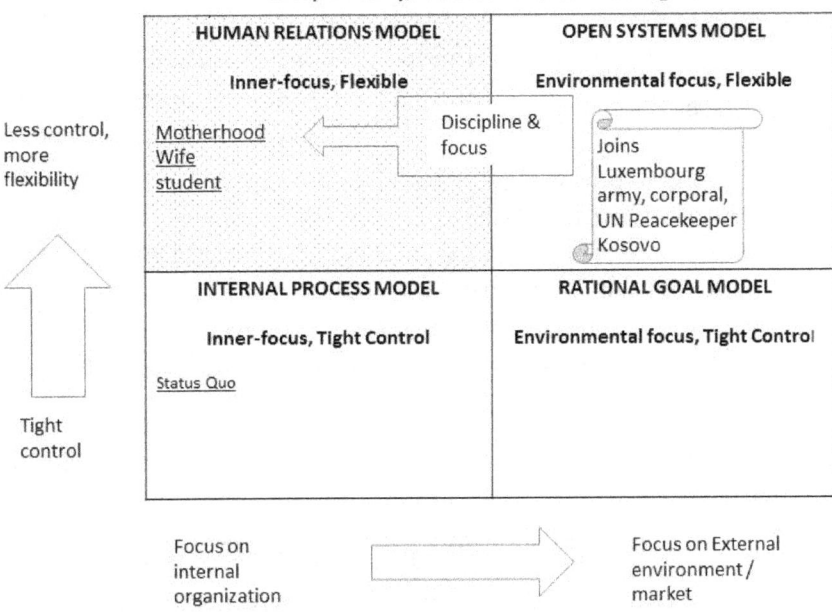

Tessy Antony, motherhood & marriage...

A year later, they added another boy to the family, Noah de Nassau. On Luxembourg's National Day celebrations on June 23, 2009, the Grand Duke gave Tessy the title of HRH Princess of Luxembourg and of Bourbon Parma and the two sons that of HRH Prince de Nassau.

B. Her Challenges

The compulsion of the Enneagram 7 Promoter is to do whatever necessary to alleviate an intense fear of the 3 Fs (FOMO, FOBLO, FOGKO), of being cast out adrift by important people.

The Seven eats everything but digests nothing, according to Tom Condon, sampling the big buffet of life, flitting here and there and then moving on. Karen Webb writes that they are 'hard to pin down to a committed schedule or work' but they are good for short-term projects with needed intense injections of work.

By outrunning pain, they only escalate the inevitable negative feedback, bad experiences, and depressing thoughts, and do not enjoy the present reality. This motivation to seek out future and dodge the negative keeps the Enneagram 7 from developing deep self awareness.

> "… there is no way to completely do away with the ego and still survive. The only viable alternative is to follow a less radical course, and make sure that one gets to know one's self, and understand its peculiarities. It is then possible to separate those needs that really help us navigate through life, from those malignant growths that sprout from them and make our lives miserable.
>
> "Once we realize what our demons are, we need not fear them any longer." (Csikszentmihalyi, 1998)

The Enneagram 7 Promoter's craving for the avoidance of pain is she often has a hard time with developing discipline and focus. Often the discipline is associated with predictable routine and limits, which the Enneagram 7 thinks of closing off options and restricting freedom of choice. Until she can come to terms with the inevitability of pain and can therefore stop avoiding it, she will continue to repeat her mistakes. For Sarah Ferguson, it was a pattern of stockpiling debt and facing bankruptcy.

> (Sarah Ferguson) explained: "I felt that I ostracized myself by my behavior, by the past, by living with all the regrets of my mistakes, that I sort of wore a hair shirt and beat myself up most of the day thinking and regretting why did I make such a mistake? Why have I made so many mistakes?" (US Weekly staff, 2011)

Outdistance the shadow of pain that shadows all of us. If you have ever avoided having 'that painful conversation', you probably tried all the following: made sure you did not cross paths with that person, you changed the subject, you hogged the conversation, you slipped out to use the washroom, you told them you are too busy to talk about that, you say it is someone else's business. It is a party and why talk about something that will get you down? It is not the right time or place to talk about it. And if the other person persists, then you cut them off. Sometimes you cut them out of your life.

> "(The) package-deal gift of human being... emits life-long warning signals when my attention is deadly to the well-being of self and others. (Shreenan, 2011)

i.   Ghosting: Someone I used to know

The phenomenon of ghosting is when someone disappears from your life and you have no idea what happened. It boils down to that person does not see a future relationship and has decided to unilaterally pull the plug. The torch song by Human League *Don't You Want Me* by Jo Callis; Philip Oakey; Philip Adrian Wright, cuts to the chase of what Enneagram 7 Promoters deploy from their repertoire: cutting loose.

Coincidentally, all three Enneagram 7 Promoter women – Princess Tessy, Meghan Markle, Sarah Ferguson - decided to terminate their first marriages around the age of 30. For Sarah Ferguson, she had enough of living in the royal court of contempt since age 26. Sarah Ferguson has made it widely known (Piers Morgan (CNN.com, 2011), Oprah Winfrey (Oprah Winfrey Show, 2011), (Sales, 2011)) that Andrew's service in the Royal Navy left her spending barely 40 days a year with her husband. And most of the time, royal duties took up time and energy. That was unbearable for a new 26 year old bride to navigate a demanding new role without a marital home of their own or the presence of Andrew 'my man'. She had enough and that was it.

Goyte with Kimbra's *Someone that I used to know* by Afika Nxumalo and Walter Andre De Backer in song and video (Gotyemusic, 2011) expresses some of the shock and bitterness felt by the recipient to this abrupt termination of a relationship. But the initiator has already thought it through and the Enneagram 7 Promoter has already moved on. Andrew Morton claims Meghan Markle mailed her wedding rings to her first husband, Trevor Engelson, from Toronto. (Canada Post offers regular mail as well as secure XpressPost service to the US – thank you, Andrew Morton, for the shout out.)

After six years of living together in Los Angeles and three years of a long distance relationship between Los Angeles and filming TV series Suits in Toronto, her first marriage to Trevor Engelson had run its course and she called time on it. It happens. (Don't blame Canada!)

A friend of 25 years, Adam Goldworm, also commented on the break-up. 'Nobody, including Trevor, knows whether there was actually anything going on,' he says, adding that the divorce had been 'her decision, totally out of the blue'. (Jones, 2018)

Trevor Engelson refuses to talk about his first wife, Meghan: 'I have zero to say about her,' he tells inquirers, icily. (Jones, 2018).

Ghosting also happens in other types of relationships including friendships and business ties. Meghan Markle went quiet on Reitmans (Hamilton, 2017) as well as her former agent, Gina Nelthorpe-Cowne. During a trip to Ottawa to attend a One Young World event in September 2016, Gina said Meghan gave her a "bit of a difficult time". And the last time she emailed her friend, Gina claims she got a reply from Meghan's lawyers.

For most Enneagram 7 Promoters, there is a sense of calling time on what is not working and then 'likes to move on' (Clarke-Billings, 2018), and her half-brother and half-sister were pointedly not invited to the wedding (Forsyth, 2018). Disgruntled and embarrassed, they are by taking it to the press and her half-sister Samantha is still talking about Meghan being vindictive (Green, 2018) and other shortcomings, even after the wedding (Koubaridis, 2018). With only Meghan's yoga teacher mother, Doria Ragland, invited her wedding to Prince Harry, half-brother Thomas Jnr publicly denounced the exclusion of Markle siblings, cousins, aunts and uncles:

> 'Meg likes to portray herself as a humanitarian, a people's person and a charitable person, but she's none of those things to her family,' Thomas said. 'She's clearly forgotten her roots and her family. Maybe the normal American family she has is embarrassing to her.' (Platell, 2018)

Her former best friend from childhood, Ninaki Priddy offered,

> 'All I can say now is that I think Meghan was calculated — very calculated — in the way she handled people and relationships. She is very strategic in the way she cultivates circles of friends. Once she decides you're not part of her life, she can be very cold. 'It's this shutdown mechanism she has. There's nothing to negotiate. She's made her decision and that's it.' (Hardy, 2017)

As for Princess Tessy, she had just graduated with a bachelor's degree from Richmond, the American University in London, and starting on a master's degree from the SOAS School of Oriental and African Studies, University of London, and her two sons were in school full time. After a decade in the Human Relations Model and developing how to juggle multiple responsibilities of motherhood and wife to Prince Louis, she was experienced in keeping things under control and was ready to widen her horizons via the Rational Goal quadrant. (To mark this transition, I have added the song *It's Amazing* by Jem to the figure below.)

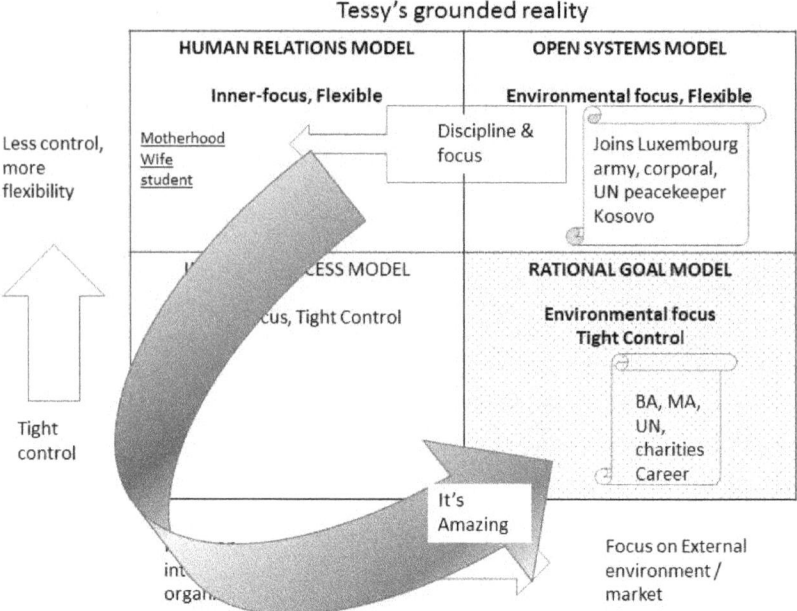

ii. Curb Your Enthusiasm: Livin' la Vida Loca

A peripatetic lifestyle, a personal history littered with relationship detritus, and overemoting are too closely associated with the flightiness and vacuity. Princess Tessy posts quite frequently on Instagram and people have wondered if she should pay more attention to personal security and privacy of her sons. The Enneagram 7 gets a bad rap for Livin la vida loca, a broken emotional thermometer, and most damning, a general lack of gravitas, not obviously burdened by intellect (Hall C., 1992). We all know what happened to royal Marie Antoinette when that reputation with taxpayers stuck to her.

> People seem much more suspicious of Markle's success as an *actual* actor, worrying that it calls her authenticity into question. When she looks so lovingly at Harry on television, how can we tell she isn't acting? On television, hasn't she just walked down the aisle with another man, looking every

bit as adoring? (Brown C. , 2018)

Meghan Markle's engagement interview has been criticized for her sounding like an airhead California valley girl, not a Northwestern University graduate. She overused 'incredible' during the engagement interview – seven times in the interview including three times in her answer on meeting the Queen. Other jargon include three times the use of some variation of 'passion/passionate'. She and Prince Harry used 'amazing' three times each in the interview.

> Former Private Secretary to Elizabeth II, Michael Charteris is quoted: "The trouble with behaving like everyone else is that you get treated like everyone else. The queen has succeeded because she has never done that." (Borrill, 1996)

Jan Moir says about Meghan Markle needing to rein it in after she is married to Harry:

> "Perhaps she doesn't mean to, but in public she frequently slips into glutinous actress mode, as if she were rather hammily playing herself in some future episode of TV's *The Crown* ... Too many layers of the custard of compassion on this particular royal trifle is going to make us all feel a little bit sick." (Brown C. , 2018)

Another example of lack of emotional regulation is Sarah Ferguson going public in 2011 about not being invited to Prince William and Catherine Middleton's wedding at Westminster Abbey. (Most people would not think the ex-wife of the groom's uncle would be included in a wedding anyways.)

With the laser focus on her own feelings, Sarah Ferguson was remarkably unfiltered, and it was all too obvious that it was not missing the bride and groom exchanging vows that disappointed her but not being part of the fun. She spoke to Oprah Winfrey about her great disappointment in missing getting her daughters Princess Beatrice and Princess Eugenie dressed and ready.

> "I wanted to be there with my girls and … to be getting them dressed and to go as a family," Ferguson said on "Oprah." "And also it was so hard because the last bride up that aisle was me." (Marikar, 2011)

She also dropped a clanger in saying,

> "And I really love the feeling that sort of Diana and I both weren't there," Ferguson told Winfrey. (US Weekly staff, 2011)

About Enneagram 7 Promoter Princess in her compulsion, she can be extremely candid and unfiltered! In the 2011 Oprah Winfrey 6-part series *Finding Sarah* , Sarah Ferguson was seen as exploiting her daughters' distress when she allowed the film crew to capture the princesses in tears; (English, Blubbing Fergie hits a new low: Duchess allows Beatrice and Eugenie to be filmed clearly in distress for latest TV series, 2011)

> "…(T)he personality's attempt to protect us stop helping. We unconsciously expect every situation and relationship to conform to our personality's special strategy. We automatically enact that strategy, even when it isn't appropriate. This prevents us from participating in the world as it actually is. So the ultimate goal of learning about your personality type is to transcend its trappings. It's to deal with your shadows." (Robertson, 2018)

The Enneagram 7 Promoters often find routine work boring and rather than delegate it out, sits on it. Attending to the excitement of the highly-entertaining big picture at the expense of the boring but critical routine tasks can trip up the Enneagram 7 Promoter Princess. When you neglect the taxman and finances – as in Sarah Ferguson (Watt, Pegg, Garside, & Bengtsson, 2016) – or get too consumed over the intricacies of a second splashy wedding, like Meghan, sometimes the black swan of blood relations are chickens coming to roost (Fraser & Holden, 2018).

They eventually respect for the institutional memory of experienced courtiers and professionals who have a deep bench of staff. Having someone to oversee the details will prevent this kind of reaction to the B-list of wedding guests to Harry and Meghan's wedding:

> "Twelve-hundred hand-picked "ordinary" people, many from charities that the royals support, will be let into the castle's grounds. They will be there for hours and hours, and yet, it seems, they will not get so much as a vol-au-vent. Those who work with deprived and alienated people have been advised in letters from lord lieutenants "to bring a picnic lunch as it will not be possible to buy food and drink on site". What? What kind of invite is that? These ordinary people will effectively be extras for the TV coverage. They'll make up a crowd that will be beamed around the world... I can't see it as anything other than meanness. Have a party or don't...
>
> Harry and Meghan's 600 actual guests will get the works, but the people chosen because they serve the most vulnerable in their communities will be left milling about for hours and are now Googling Windsor for the nearest supermarkets.
>
> As a metaphor for inclusivity royal-style, though, it's all perfect, isn't it? Do please come and gawp and cheer, but bring your own sandwiches. The meanness of the super-rich is truly something to behold." (Moore, 2018)

That kind of attention to unpleasant tasks would have spared Meghan and Harry the 'Markle debacle' the week before the wedding in which Thomas Markle's staged paparazzi collusion photos and his attendance-non-attendance-attendance- back and forth looked like a wedding planner's nightmare (Kay & Levy, Feuding palace courtiers are whispering about the 'Markle debacle' but are they to blame or is it control-freak Harry, asks RICHARD KAY, 2018)

iii. Reinventing: Raindrops keep fallin on my head

An Enneagram 7 Promoter Princess changes the channel constantly, sometimes commitment phobic, always on the look out for the positive spin. BJ Thomas's version of the Oscar-winning song, Raindrops keep fallin on my head, from 1969's *Butch Cassidy and the Sundance Kid* by the team of Hal David and Burt Bacharach correlates on how the Promoter wants to make lemonade from a crop of lemons.

Intense bursts of energy and laser sharp focus for short projects is preferred as the Promoter does not want to tied down. Princess Tessy speaks to how she goes about managing work by seasons in a podcast interview with Haniel Vidmar (Haniel Vidmar, 2018)

On Friday May 18, the day before the wedding, her recuperating father Thomas Markle spoke to TMZ: "…says Meghan and Harry told him they had no plans to visit him. He told them he hoped to travel to the UK to meet Harry and see Meghan "sometime in the near future." (TMZ, 2018).

This may seem at odds to the purported closeness between father and daughter but from the point of view of Enneagram 7 Promoter Princess, it is a recalibration. Now that the **heated** discussion over his attendance is finally over, and his cardiac health is on the mend, there is no reason for Meghan and Harry to alter their honeymoon plans and rush to his bedside. Things can revert to normal.

When it comes to getting an accurate read on a Promoter, even the mighty New York Times found Sarah Ferguson, the subject of *Finding Sarah*, as slippery as a fish:

> "The tantalizing thing about "Finding Sarah," the Duchess of **York**'s six-part voyage of self-discovery beginning Sunday

on OWN, is that not even **Oprah Winfrey** can pin her down. The disgraced, debt-plagued Sarah Ferguson confronts her guilt, shares her pain, seeks her personal truth, consults a shaman, hikes in the Arctic and emerges redeemed and ready for her book tour… without ever having to address directly what she offered a tabloid reporter posing as a businessman last year in exchange for £500,000... (A hidden camera showed Ms. Ferguson promising access to her former husband, Prince Andrew, who is a trade envoy for Britain.)

Instead, Ms. Ferguson smothers the unsavory subject in a thick eiderdown of self-esteem issues like "self-sabotage" and a "people-pleasing addiction." She didn't spend her way into debt, Ms. Ferguson realizes, she gave away too much to too many people because of her "overgenerous" nature.

And that alone suggests that the oft-ridiculed Duchess of York is actually a marketing savant who could teach Ms. Orman a thing or two." (Stanley, 2011)

"I changed my mind" or "It was a jest" is the common response when asked to justify an egregious statement. One example is Sarah Ferguson's comments regarding her mother in the first episode of the 2011 *Finding Sarah* series. She claims her mother, Susan Barrantes, regularly beat her:

> "'When she used to hit me because I didn't sit on my potty or wouldn't eat, a little vein would come up on the centre of my head near my red hair.' It was this vein that her mother dubbed the 'sign of the devil' as she tried to beat it out of her." (Daily Mail, 2011) .

And this Susan's approach to toilet training toddler Sarah:

> "And on one occasion, she tied Sarah, who was on the potty, to the leg of a table while lunching with friends in the dining room next door.

> Dr Phil commented that 'lashing a kid to a table ... was not OK'.
>
> To which Fergie says she replied: 'Well, no wonder I'm so flawed.' (Levy, 2011)

A few days later, on June 9, 2011 her older sister, Jane Ferguson spoke from Sydney, Australia:

> "I don't remember that verbal abuse, but that's Sarah's experience." "She's not lying, that's her experience, but my experience was that Mum was a wonderful woman and loved us both enormously and did the best she could." (Malkin, 2011).

At the end of July 2011, after the 6-episode series finished airing, Sarah Ferguson clarified in an interview for Hello! that there was no abuse from her mother (Churcher, 2011). Sarah Ferguson rationalizes her inaccurate statements:

> "Posing for a photo by her mother's grave, the Duchess elaborated on her beating allegation: 'She didn't actually do that . . . she probably smacked my bottom a couple of times.... 'I was just being light-hearted...'

iv. Uninhibited Rebel: Grease is the word

Anand Subhuti has posted his opinion of Meghan as Enneagram 3 The Worker Bee Achiever. There is definitely a case made for that; however, I would offer that Meghan Markle's actions indicate more closely Enneagram 7 Promoter Princess. Both personality styles have high energy and like to make a difference. The main difference is in the reaction to authority – the 3 respects it; the 7 rebels against it.

As Barry Gibb says, "Grease is the word."

https://www.youtube.com/watch?v=JhrPTu-1kSI

Subhuti himself predicts that once she enters the royal family as Harry's wife that Meghan would 'resent its limitations'. That statement alone of visceral recoil from rules and 'the way things are done' is the trademark of the 7 Promoter. The Promoter feels anxiety with the ceding of control to others as that indicates closing off unlimited options. Enneagram 3 would be on board with the rules and make the rulebook serve her own goals.

This is apparent from the beginning of the engagement. Meghan Markle as fiancée keeps one foot outside the royal camp in both her first official set of photos and her first appearance with the extended royal family. Released shortly before Christmas 2017, the portraits by New York-based fashion photographer Alexi Lubomirski allude to a glamorous celebrity couple rather than a crumpets-and-tea royal couple of earlier days. Moreover, she chose to make a statement in that conventionally rite of passage official engagement photo session. She went bra-less. And the sheer bodice Ralph & Russo gown retails at eyewatering $75,000. Ostensibly a portrait of a couple, it is blindingly clear that she eclipses Prince Harry. He is reduced to arm candy. (Sarah Ferguson did the same to Prince Andrew, with her larger-than-life persona in the 1986 engagement interview.)

Leaving church after Christmas 2017 service, Meghan stuck her tongue out at well-wishers. That is an audacious sign of her uninhibited playfulness even on a holy day in the Christian calendar.

Since then, it has been her messy bun with two tendrils hanging that captures attention. Even at her wedding at St George's, Windsor, a tendril made a special appearance.

The Enneagram 3 princess just does not throw caution to the winds, 'messy' messes up her image. Think the Crown Princess of Denmark, née Mary Donaldson, whose poised demeanor at her own engagement seem consistent with Enneagram 3. Only a couple years prior to the engagement to Prince Frederik, she was obviously bra-less with him at a wedding (Hola, 2003). But since then, she has 'hoisted those sisters up' and kept things covered.

Enneagram 3 Worker Bee would agree with William Hanson, etiquette expert, on a seated wedding banquet with porcelain plates. No doubt it is trendy to have bowl food for the wedding reception, and that is what Prince Harry and Meghan Markle have in store for their guests (Naylor, 2018).

The two weeks prior to the May 19 wedding ie the 'Markle debacle' solidified Meghan Markle fitting more accurately the Enneagram 7 Promoter Princess. An Enneagram 3 simply does not have loose ends this close to the ceremony – in fact, she simmered down problematic relations that come with blended families (Steafel, 2018) prior to the engagement. Loose cannons are vocal in their disappointment and vocal about it to all and sundry (TMZ, 2018) but there is merit to having them on your side, as Lyndon B Johnson spoke of Edgar J Hoover: "Well, it's probably better to have him inside the tent pissing out, than outside pissing in." (Halberstam, 1971) .

No way would an Enneagram 3 let her adored 73-year old father not meet the groom earlier (Lusher, Is Thomas Markle's story of whether to attend the royal wedding a 'rollercoaster of speculation' or a cruel soap opera?, 2018). Just what good reason did Prince Harry have for not taking his British diplomatic passport and his fiancée onto a jet to Baja California anytime in the two years leading up to the wedding? (Treble, 2018). Had Harry been proactive the Father Markle debacle in the week leading up to the wedding could have been avoided (Morgan, Why Meghan, Harry and the clueless Palace may come to rue the day they left the backstabbing, money-grabbing Markles out in the cold and turned this wedding into a right royal tacky mess, 2018).

It would have more fitting for this 73-year old senior citizen to have an extended visit with his daughter prior to the wedding (Kay & Levy, Feuding palace courtiers are whispering about the 'Markle debacle' but are they to blame or is it control-freak Harry, asks RICHARD KAY, 2018) rather than a 'fly-in-fly-out' cameo appearance of walking his 37-year old divorced daughter down the aisle (Maloney, 2018) with 8-hour time-difference jetlag.

An anonymous palace source has offered that Meghan Markle and

Sarah Ferguson are similar in terms of personality and outlook. (Spector, 2018) The Enneagram 7 Promoter Princess personality feels free to talk without filters "a remarkable readiness to spill her guts about herself" (Pukas, 2007). She is comfortable letting it all hang out in these types of physical expressions and gestures. People may recall seeing the taped interview of her March 1986 engagement to Prince Andrew (later the Duke of York), during which Sarah Ferguson rolled her eyes and made faces to the camera. (DeYoung, 1986). Happy at getting married, the new Duchess of York nodded and smiled at friends while walking down the wedding aisle. (Moir, 2009) In support of charity, she threw herself wholeheartedly June 17, 1987 into the spirit of Prince Edward's *It's a Royal Knockout* televised team tournament (Holmquist, 2010).

The natural expressiveness of the Duchess of York, a full-blown Enneagram 7 Promoter Princess, gleefully heedless of protocol 'Fergie, who was seen as a protocol-flaunting party girl' (Jordan, 2009), resonated badly with the royal courtiers and conservative members of the public a generation ago. (Roseman, 1996)

> The Grand Royal It's A Knockout TV programme was a disaster, in which she played an important role. She horsed around, she fell about. The Princess Royal and Prince Andrew retained a modicum of decorum. The duchess did not. For royal commentators it was a key moment. The duchess was a good time girl, a podgy youngster who may have been good for a laugh but in the end was a joke herself.
>
> It was a critical turning point, says Ben Pimlott, author of the recent biography of Queen Elizabeth. "The duchess was whisked into a show business world. Nobody was prepared for it and she was not prepared for it." The duchess admits that the "public relations debacle would be analysed as my first great blunder". (Ahmed, 1996)

This push-the-envelope quality of the Enneagram 7 Promoter Princess that characterize Enneagram 7 Promoters like Tessy, Sarah, and Meghan some people have said made them acceptable for the younger son. But if the elder had produced any of them as prospective bride, well, too risky. "She will never be queen," so they are fine for those down the line of succession.

My response is only, "Things happen." The Duke and Duchess of Cambridge prefer to travel with their entire family, flying together for 2017 tour of British Colombia and the Yukon, breaking the rules with impunity and throwing caution to the winds (AOL.com editors, 2017). Prince William's great-aunt and most of her family died in a plane crash. In 1937, Prince Philip, the Duke of Edinburgh, lost his youngest sister, Princess Cecile of Greece, and his brother-in-law, George Donatus Grand Duke of Hesse-Darmstadt, and their two sons while enroute to London for the wedding of George's brother. (Eade, 2017)

On a much smaller scale of pushing-the-envelope, Princess Tessy of Luxembourg has similarly been criticized for mixing her advocacy work as a princess with promoting products and services as brand ambassador, particularly on social media such as her Instagram feed. It can be argued in her defence, however, that most of her posts focus on her public speaking engagements and advocacy on behalf of disempowered women, AIDS, and the charity she co-founded, Professors without Borders (Barger, EXCLUSIVE: Tessy Antony, Princess of Luxembourg talks charity work, 2018). It seems that she wants to connect with likeminded people who are active online and a young single simply exercising her freedom of speech.

C. Enneagram 7 Promoter Shoe: Gladiator Stiletto

When the Promoter princess is about to promote something, a cause or The Firm, she requires a shoe that matches her personality and makes a statement. In the spotlight, The Promoter princess knows nothing can attract the eye of the camera better than a stiletto. A woman who can rock a gladiator and a stiletto is comfortable and confident in the full glare of publicity.

Sarah Ferguson spots a stiletto and a riding crop in Harper's Bazaar (Wilson, 2007)

http://i.dailymail.co.uk/i/pix/2007/02_1/harpersPA_400x929.jpg

Meghan Markle knows that Hollywood likes to see thigh, toenail polish, and the leggy leanness and has maintained this look ever since (Effervescence Media, 2018).

http://meghansmirror.com/wp-content/uploads/2018/01/Meghan-Markle-Carolinna-Espinosa.jpg

Princess Tessy dresses the part at the 2017 He for She Heroes Award charity dinner in a stunning white gown and stilettos (RTL.lu, 2017) http://africanglitz.com/wp-content/uploads/2017/10/22489944_1566497550060034_30283083 7499704963_n.jpg and this 2016 Black & White ball http://snap361.com/ig-post/1352298422736502199_1993316956 and a summer party the same year:
https://www.pinterest.co.uk/pin/458733912027413482/

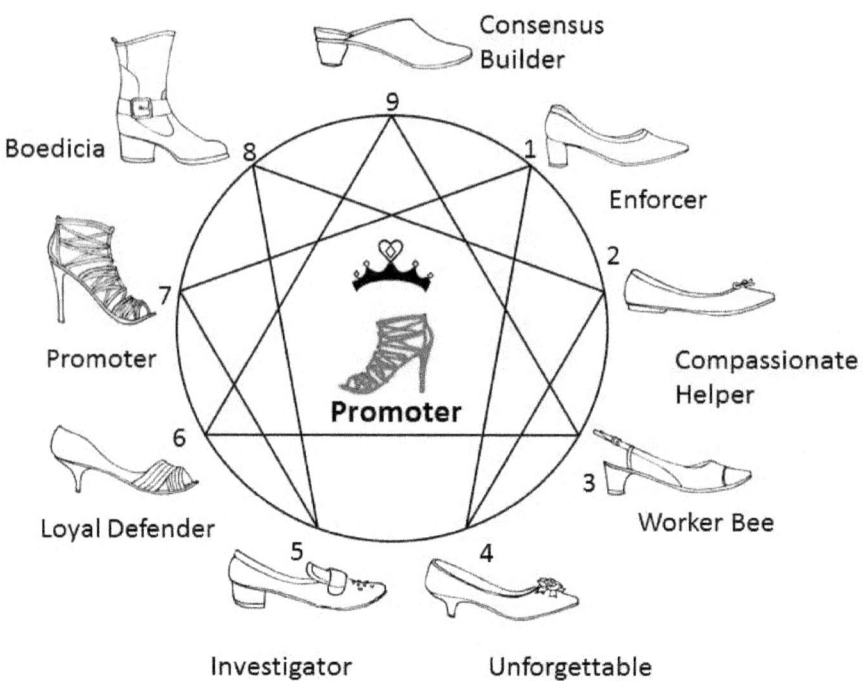

5. Enneagram 7 Promoter: Subtypes

Wait, there's more…

The Enneagram postulates that there are 9 life strategies. Each of these nine strategies that inform personality reach differently at the instinctual level, three subtypes to each personality style. Beatrice Chestnut writes authoritatively on subtypes; she paraphrases Claudio Naranjo's description of personality style subtypes thus: 'subtype expresses a compulsion – or as Naranjo puts it, a neurotic need – which is an insatiable need that drives behavior forcefully at the instinctual level.'

As for Naranjo's explanation on the instinctual level, she describes it as 'an instinctual level that encompasses and reflects the pervasiveness of three goals of human instinctual behavior – survival (the self-preservation instinct), relationships (the social instinct), and pleasure (the sexual or one-to-one instinct) (Chestnut, Enneagram Theory: The 'State of the Art' of Enneagram Subtypes, 2010).

Tom Condon is one of several Enneagram writers who refers to Margaret Frings Keyes's pithy words for subtypes "with the phrase "the One, the Few and the Many." That is how the Enneagram 7 Promoter Princess keeps fear at bay and focuses attention on keeping positive, keeping up (high energy level), and keeping going (future focus): The one ideal relationship (intimate) or Us Happy Few in the know (self-preservation) and on the go or We are in this together (social).

All the Enneagram 7 Promoter princesses are involved in charities and how she approaches it reflects her subtype. Sarah Ferguson founded her charity for children, Children in Crisis, and it is very much about her and her daughters, a very Intimate subtype setup. Meghan Markle's charities are all well-established, high profile, which provide opportunities to meet well-connected people, that is how the Self-

Preservation subtype selects charity work. Tessy Antony and two friends cofounded Professors without Borders from the ground up, having identified an unmet need. It welcomes people from a variety of backgrounds to participate, and there are bios for each founder and team member. This is very much how a Social subtype finds charity work fulfilling, a crowd approach.

Enneagram 7 Subtypes

FOCUS	SUBTYPE	EXAMPLE
One-to-One	Intimate	Sarah (Ferguson), Duchess of York
Select Few	Self-Preservation	Meghan Markle
Many	Social	Tessy Antony de Nassau, Princess of Luxembourg

A. *Focus on The One: Intimate Subtype*

Sarah Ferguson's behavior is very Seven according to Enneagram authors Michael Goldberg and Tom Condon. The Intimate subtype of the Enneagram 7 Promoter seeks refuge from anxiety of limits in an idealized Other for a rejuvenation and renewal. As per the hit by The Stylistics, "You make me feel brand new"
https://www.youtube.com/watch?v=Yu1Ezr1YEoY
This could be a romantic partner or a mentor figure. In this, Sarah Ferguson has a pattern, in the full glare of the media, of searching for this ideal through the years.

She idealizes her men - the determinedly-single widower Paddy McNally, Prince Andrew RN, John Bryan, the married Italian count Gaddo della Gherardesca – and unconsciously filters in the unavailable ones – married, not the marrying kind, in the navy. Which goes a long way to blame the man for relationship failure.

About why her marriage to Prince Andrew ended: "You can't build a foundation of marriage on loneliness," she says. "And I loved Andrew, but he wasn't there to embrace.". (Burke, 2009) "Andrew was away at sea 320 days a year. I wanted my man beside me. I was an affair waiting to happen, " she told the Daily Express. Then she tried confession - "Basically, I'd done a great job of sabotaging and humiliating myself in Britain." (Pukas, 2007)

Her selection process for mentors and confidantes similarly filters out truly kind people who help but do not rescue and at the same time lets in the indiscreet who promise instant stress-relief or the easy way to bring in the bucks.

> She sought, she told the reporter, freedom from marriage, but freedom wasn't what she was educated for. (McDonaugh, 2010)

And who eventually cash in on their connection with Sarah, like her faith healer who taped their talks, Madame Vasso, and published a tell-all, *The Duchess of York: Uncensored:*

> " While Fergie was five months pregnant, she hunkered down for hanky-panky with U.S. businessman Steve Wyatt in the bushes near the Yorks' estate. She also allegedly offered sex tips to Diana. Then Vasso released audiotapes, made without permission. Last week callers to a phone hot line (shut down after less than a day) could hear Fergie fantasizing about JFK Jr., rating her eight lovers (Wyatt was the best) and bad-mouthing the royal family. ""I want to see deaths," she says with a giggle. Now the duchess is considering a lawsuit against Vasso for invasion of privacy. **(Newsweek, 1996)**

Unappreciated, Sarah was consistently described by confidantes who later wrote tell-all books on her as 'insecure, oversexed, self-destructive' (Kennedy, 1996)

In her idealization of someone glamorously fun with a trendy lifestyle to the point of overlooking very unhealthy qualities, the Intimate subtype would be prone to things like this quotation from the Oscar-winning film *Gigi*: "I'd rather be miserable with you than without you." (IMDb.com, 2018)

> Royal commentator, Dickie Arbiter, told ITV's 'The Royal Wives of Windsor': "Okay you don't expect somebody to crawl through the bushes to take photographs of you topless while your financial advisor is sucking your toes. "You don't expect that but by the same token you don't go away with somebody that isn't your husband and sunbathe topless." (Perrring, 2018)

Allan Starkie writes about how badly John Bryan treated Sarah in their relationship and alleges it was Bryan who set up the infamous topless photos of the two in August 1992 in St Tropez.

The compulsion to bond with someone who will do the heavy lifting only delays the inner work necessary for this subtype's personal growth: there are no shortcuts to developing the skills of focus and discipline except to do it yourself. Sarah Ferguson avoided this inner work and hit rock bottom several times over the years.

B. Focus on The Few: Self-Preservation Subtype

Andrew Morton describes Meghan Markle 'supreme networker' in promoting his recently released biography "Meghan: A Hollywood Princess" (Armecin, 2018) To make it in the entertainment industry, you have to 'hustle' a term Meghan Markle and her first husband, Trevor Engelson, are said to have used in their 6 years living together in LA as a couple, a glamour couple camera-ready, working hard, and going places. I think the energy of this partnership is captured by the hit *Working for the Weekend* from the Canadian band, Loverboy: https://www.youtube.com/watch?v=zL8G5pBZ5CI

The Enneagram 7 Promoter Princess Self-Preservation subtype can have the following motto, from Steve Harvey's Twitter. He has mentioned on his show something his late father said, "Everybody that comes with you can't go with you. Always evaluate who you have "on your wagon" You'll lose friends while you're climbing to the top. Everyone will not go to the top with you!. (Harvey, 2014) Meghan Markle presents this in her actions after being cast in the cable television series *Suits*.

After living with Trevor Engelson in Los Angeles and auditioning time and again, she caught her big break just after turning 29 on August 4, 2010 when the production company released to the media on August 24, 2010 that she was cast to start filming in New York the 80-minute pilot of *A Legal Mind* (which later became *Suits*) on the USA Network. (The Futon Critic, 2010)

When the show was later picked up by the USA Network, the producers chose Toronto as the film location for the series. Thanks to Canada and Ontario's tax credits for TV and film location shots, Toronto developed a deep bench of production crew expertise and a pool of talent and soundstage space to meet the needs of production companies worldwide but particularly in the United States. TIFF, the Toronto International Film Festival, is where many Oscar-contention movies break out, with a savvy audience of local film buffs, media, and arts community (Hall A. , 2016). I even wrote a short book about the background extra work on sets all through the Toronto entertainment industry: *Standing Out in the Background: A Guide to Extra Work in Toronto's Film & TV Industry: Second Edition with Enneagram Section*

In addition, the Greater Toronto Area (GTA) has a reputation of being a friendly and clean place to live, a global city with a connected financial district, major league sports like hockey, baseball, and basketball, and part of the nation's technology hub, a nexus of the type Richard Florida calls the creative class in a superstar city. Two wine regions are within 2 hours drive: Niagara and Prince Edward County. The variety of Chinese cuisine in Toronto rivals the best served San Francisco, Singapore, and Vancouver. In the second decade of the millennium, every year it seems someone from Toronto is in the zeitgeist – Rob Ford the late mayor, Drake the hometown star, Margaret Atwood the writer, Jordan Peterson of the University of Toronto.

After she relocated to Toronto for *Suits* and later marrying Trevor Engelson in a four-day destination wedding in Jamaica, the couple never lived together again. Long distance does not work, according to Thomas Hodges of doclove.com, (Hodges, 2018) and they divorced and each moved on.

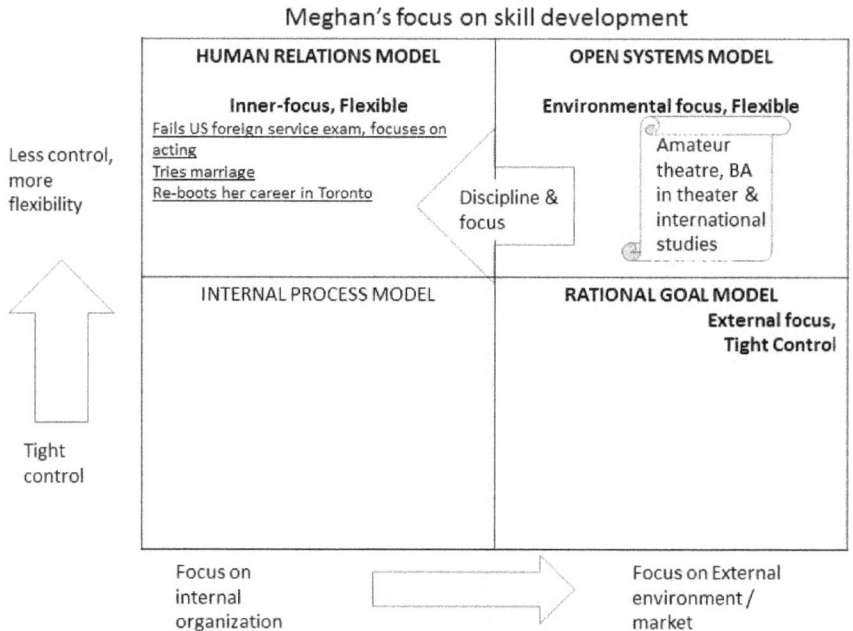

It makes sense that she made the best of her starring role in a new city, to reinvent herself now that she was single for the first time since she met Trevor Engelson. Although it is not Hollywood in terms of the significance of its entertainment industry, Toronto has many advantages that a one-industry town like Los Angeles simply does not have. In Canada, Toronto used to be called Hog Town, the nation's confluence of industry, law, banking, higher education, performing arts, media, technology (Marche, 2016). For Meghan Markle to make social connections quickly in Canada, it is easier from the vantage point of *Suits* doing many location shoots in the finest restaurants and hotels and shops in downtown Toronto. And being legally single makes her available to the social scene in the city, wiping the slate clean alleviates the 3 Fs (FOMO, FOBLO, FOGKO). Being in relationship with celebrity chef Cory Vitiello introduced her to influential Torontonians in the media and led to her charity work in soup kitchens, World Vision Canada, among others. (Szklarski, 2018)

Canadians by and large do not lose their common sense in the midst of celebrities, a lack of paparazzi culture that Andrew Morton believes allowed Prince Harry and Meghan Markle to date quietly (Toronto Life, 2018). Amanda Dishaw of the blog Meghan's Mirror (with Christine O'Brien" says Canadian readers are convinced "she came into her own while living in Toronto" (Murphy, 2017)

Meghan laid the ground for making it easy for Harry to propose by showing that Self-Preservation subtype knows the game and the rules, which the Intimate Enneagram 7 Promoter Princess subtype Sarah Ferguson did not regard highly enough.

> "…she is more famous and more influential than she was ever likely to be on her own. It remains the way of the world. Does Amal Clooney have more resources as a human rights lawyer and philanthropist now that she is married to George Clooney? No doubt." (Jefferson, 2018)

The game is that those of the inner circle of The Firm do not keep lifestyle blogs nor tweet and Meghan Markle shut hers down. She also adopted dress that is more in line with a royal ambassadorial role, while keeping some elements of her personality.

> Which is why other supposed fashion faux pas, such as Markle's now signature messy bun or her penchant for cross-

body purses instead of clutch bags (leaving her arms free to hug well-wishers in the crowds), could instead be read as a way of communicating her personality now that she can no longer rely on speaking directly to fans on social media or her lifestyle blog, the Tig, which she shuttered ahead of the engagement announcement last year. (Yossman, 2018)

The Enneagram 7 Promoter Self-Preservation subtype cares deeply for those who are in her network. The message and the team and her closely-guarded Happy Few in her new network are all on point (Watson, 2018) and prominent seating at the wedding in Windsor. With adverse publicity in the media, this inner circle is vulnerable to getting overconfident - Royal commenter Rupert Bell warns that controlling the story is not always possible, can lead to frustration – and cautions against a British Kardashian scenario. (Scotto Di Santolo, 2018)

Black Swan situations can arise from unexpected sources and from those outside the network. For those on the periphery, one might as well be on Pluto as her own father Thomas Markle found it easier to confide his intentions to attend her wedding, and his changes of mind, to TMZ.com than his own daughter and the future son-in-law he has not yet met (Sykes, How TMZ Crashed Meghan Markle and Prince Harry's Wedding. Devastatingly., 2018)

C. Focus on The Many: The Social Subtype

The instinctual drive of the Enneagram 7 Promoter Social subtype is on involvement with the many. Unlike Intimate subtype who craves bonding with an Other and the Self-Preservation who wants a select group of well-connected people, the Social subtype finds meaning in the working with a large part of the populace, serving the greater good.

In 2003, at age 18, freshly graduated from high school, Tessy signed up for the Luxembourg Army (Barger, EXCLUSIVE: Tessy Antony, Princess of Luxembourg talks life, education, social media in two part interview, 2018). She joined her twin brother and older sister in the service, encouraged by her parents who are involved in local politics. Engaging with the external environment and having the flexibility to do so in the Open Systems quadrant is an easy decision for the Enneagram 7 Promoter.

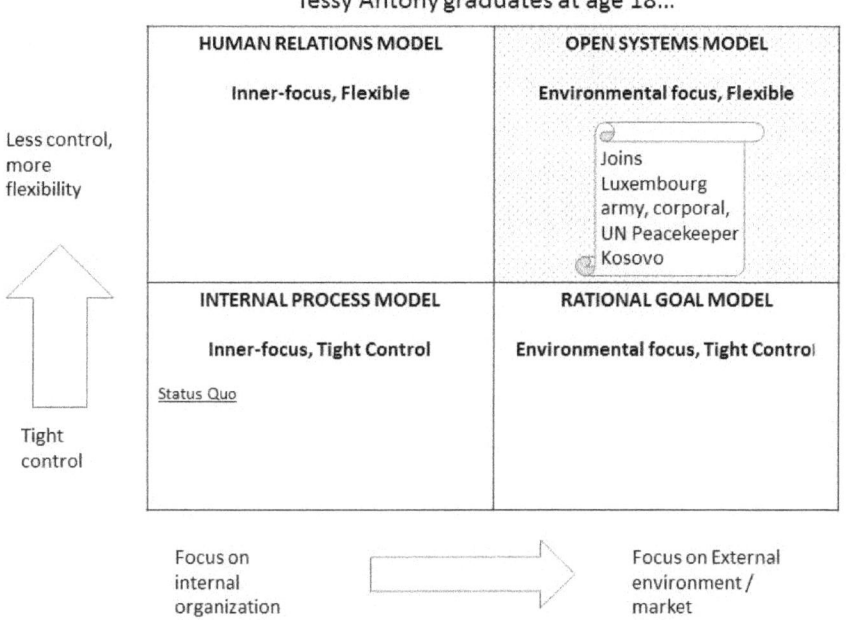

In her 5 years, she advanced to the rank of corporal (Armée luxembourgeoise, 2018) and was deployed as part of UN Peacekeeping in Kosovo (KFOR), March to August 2004 (Sawer, 2017). It was her first time travelling without her family, very much in the Open Systems quadrant. She mentions in her interview with Place Royale "Princesse Tessy sa nouvelle vie de celibataire" (RTL.be, 2017) on RTL Belgium meeting the women survivors of sexual violence, which is why she later became is a patron of UNA-UK. In a piece published in the Telegraph, she speaks frankly about what she experienced age barely 20:

> "My UN deployment is a memory that I will cherish forever. It taught me how to stay strong in difficult situations. My day-to-day job was very simple: I worked in a two-person unit that took care of logistics to support my colleagues. I drove a Hummer and a truck – or anything else to hand – and provided support during night watches, searches and other operations.
>
> But the core of my job was different. As a woman – one of very few female peacekeepers – I found that I was able to provide a service for women and girls, who suffer terribly in conflict zones. While doing night watches or searches, I was able to support them, listen to them and defend them.
>
> There were times when I, like they, wanted to escape the harsh, male-dominated environment. I also experienced a degree of attempted abuse. Luckily, I had the tools and training to defend myself. However, hundreds of thousands of women all over the world are not as fortunate. I want to speak up for them." (Tessy, 2016)

Her charity work now includes UNA-UK (UNA-UK, 2017) and UNAIDS Global Advocate for Young Women and Adolescent Girls.

6. Enneagram 7 Promoter Princess: Prison or Paradise?

Germaine Greer stated darkly in an interview about the chances of Meghan Markle lasting in the British Monarchy (Australia, 2018) "Stay with it for as long as it lasts, why not. But don't stay for the bad bit. Be prepared to go when it gets bad. Just say, 'That's it. Gave it my best shot. I'm outta here'. I think she'll bolt. She bolted before."

Other media is openly taking bets (Klein Nixon, 2018)

What can happen after I do? It depends on The Firm because the Enneagram 7 Promoter will lead with the song *Don't Fence Me In* by Robert Fletcher and Cole Porter (Youtube, 2012). Unilateral restrictions could lead to ghosting.

A. Sarah Ferguson: Don't Make Me Over

In 1992, TRH the Duke and Duchess of York decided to divorce after six years of marriage and two daughters. Sarah has attributed their marriage failure to seeing her husband a scant 40 days of the year.

The Navy Wife Life is not what Sarah had signed up for. In the engagement interview, she looked forward to being a good team with Andrew, not two people carrying on a long-distance relationship.

"I thought I was going to marry my man, go to Portland and be in naval quarters. And then I was told by the family and by the security officers that I couldn't do that. So two weeks after we got married, or three weeks, I was told, `He's going to Portland and you stay where you are.' " Andrew, she adds, "was in the same boat as I was." (Boycott, 1996)

Left alone, the victim of unrelenting media torment and a series of press leaks she attributes to the "Grey Men", she badly needed help. It was not forthcoming from the Firm. "Because the Royal Family are perfect, it must be you who's the problem." (Boycott, 1996)

Sarah herself says that the 'Grey Men', the sober courtiers of the establishment, criticized her relentlessly for not meekly conforming. It appears that the scant amount advice that was offered came across in a way that unintentionally antagonizes an Enneagram 7 Promoter Princess.

Motivating an energetic, optimistic, extrovert Enneagram 7 Promoter Princess first with dry-as-dust sessions does not inspire learning nor compliance. Feedback consisting of yelling at Sarah (she nicknamed royal courtier and cousin Robert Fellowes 'Robert Bellows') only inspires insurrection.

If the palace were to get serious about retention of newcomers, HR would need to update their training manual. That does not mean handing out University of Toronto's Professor Jordan Peterson's 2018 bestseller! An Enneagram 7 Promoter Princess would look at the title - *12 Rules for Life: An Antidote to Chaos* – and would find two issues with the title alone. The '*12 Rules*' would get a snort at the limitation of rules – for the Enneagram 7 Promoter Princess, rules are the means to stifle, restrict, and confine her energies. And as for '*Antidote for Chaos*', she would query, "So what's wrong with chaos? It is better than a 12 Rules of Stepford Wife."

Perhaps but chaos is what happens when there are no limits at all. As William Hanson advised, guidelines and plans serve a practical purpose:

> "So many people try to do weddings without a seating plan," says Hanson. "It's bonkers and it's a recipe for disaster. 'Oh I just want people to turn up and sit wherever they want'. Well, great, you will have chaos if you do it that way." (Douglas, 2018)

Better to develop a training program suited to the personality of the Enneagram 7 Promoter, honoring her potential and contributions within grounded reality. When a prince marries someone beyond his narrow social circle, he is injecting diversity of some sort into the monarchy. She needs to feel welcome and her perspectives and opinions are at least heard at the table, especially since her new role is to promote the monarchy. This is essentially co-opting her buy-in, that she has a stake in the monarchy's survival. Ensuring the new recruit has 'skin in the game' boosts feeling included, engaged, and empowered. (Smith & Turner, 2015)

What a sad waste of Sarah's natural talents. Enneagram 7 Promoter Princesses like to talk with people and when there is a spotlight, they can perform for the camera. As Sarah Ferguson indicated in her biography, the establishment tried to stifle her fundamental exuberance:

> "Their hostility toward outsiders was legend," and when they decided she would not change, actively sought to drive her out of the royal family. (Ferguson Mountbatten-Windsor Duchess of York, 1996)

It was not enough for them that she was stressed out and bankrupt, they were so determined to silence her that they threw up obstacles for her having any kind of a public life in the UK after marriage. She had start over outside of the country, and sell her life story, over and over.

> "And the story never really changes. It is always a variation on the same theme: bad Mummy left home when she was twelve, and poor Fergie hasn't quite found her self-esteem; Prince Andrew is marvellous/wonderful and would still be married to her if not for the bad 'grey men' at the Palace, plus

of course, her need to earn money to settle debts caused by her lavish spending." (Holder, 2011)

To get beyond that tired narrative, Sarah had to hit the reset button and deal with it by painful self-examination of her role in the debacle:

> In her interview with Sarah Ferguson who was promoting the film Young Victoria, Jodie Burke in the LA Times, asked: What would she do differently?
>
> Response: "Learn the game. Play it properly."
>
> Burke: Stay in the palace?
>
> "Yes," she says. "Completely." (Burke, 2009)

By her getting outplayed by the courtiers, Sarah found herself completely shut out, not invited to events like the Golden and Diamond Jubilees and William and Catherine's wedding. An Enneagram 7 Promoter Princess really does mind being excluded from the festivities, despite admitting in 2007 she had not seen William nor Harry in ten years (Pukas, 2007). She was vocal about it in an interview with Oprah Winfrey in full-blown distress at being so conspicuously and pointedly not wanted, giving into the 3 Fs of FOMO, FOBLO, FOGKO (Friedman, 2018). Nursing her disappointment in style, Sarah Ferguson headed to the Kamalaya Wellness Sanctuary luxury resort, on Koh Samui island in Thailand.

B. Princess Tessy: Is That All There Is? (No!)

On January 18, 2017, Princess Tessy confirmed an announcement from the Grand Ducal court that her marriage to Prince Louis was ending by divorce. (Mooney & Linning, 2017) A month later, the decree nisi, the next-to-last legal step to dissolution of marriage, was pronounced in London.

Money is what keeps the couple from obtaining the decree absolute at the time. Unlike Sarah Ferguson, Princess Tessy is standing up for herself to secure a decent financial settlement. Sarah, being an Enneagram 7 Promoter Princess of the Intimate subtype, valued a personal relationship with Elizabeth II. Her thinking emphasized the importance of keeping the Queen on her side or at least not be cast out of the court by HM. To the Enneagram 7 Promoter Princess, the fear of being left out (FOBLO) from the action is cannot be overstated as a source of anxiety:

> When the inevitable divorce took place, Sarah says she 'opted for friendship' rather than money from the Royal Family. She writes: 'Her Majesty asked me: "What do you require, Sarah?" And I said: "Your friendship," which I think amazed her, because everyone said I would demand a big settlement.' (Levy, 2011)

And so Sarah admits having settled for much less than her legal team could have negotiated for, sacrificing financially to her FOBLO.

> Thanks to some misplaced notion that she still had a relationship with the Queen worth preserving, Fergie was persuaded by royal lawyers into walking away from her marriage with no house, no income, and an unbelievably paltry £15,000-a-year settlement. (Brown T. , 2010)

Friendship with the queen is all well and good but Sarah still remained persona non grata in court. What she had not fully taken into account is that Elizabeth II is queen but it is Prince Philip who is head of the household. And he does not want to see Sarah at all, which Sarah has stated meant she has not spent Christmas with her daughters in years as the princesses leave with Andrew and his family, despite the huge concession in the divorce settlement, she was still Kicked Out.

> "Sarah found herself denied access to the big house at Sandringham. Determined to be close to the children, she elected to stay at the gate house. Cars were sent for Eugenie and Beatrice early in the morning. Andrew entertained his daughters, leaving his wife alone like a dog in quarantine." (Boycott, 1996)

So set against Sarah is Prince Phillip that even Her Majesty has to see Sarah 'on the sly'. (Linning, 2014)

By contrast, Tessy has the goal of securing the financial future for her sons and herself, a testament of the social drive of this Enneagram 7 Promoter Princess subtype. She does not stint in seeking justice, retaining top divorce lawyer, Deborah Bangay QC, of 1 Hare Court (1 Hare Court, 2018). The thinking core of the Enneagram 7 Promoter Princess summed up that a fair financial settlement was more important than anything that critics and pundits could throw at her. To counter the accusations of being a gold digger in the scurrilous press, Tessy even sought to make public the financial settlement she proposed ([2017] EWHC 3095 (Fam), 2017). (The matter is now making its way towards some sort of resolution, sooner rather than later.)

Regarding the gold digger label: Princess Tessy had benefited from her marriage to Prince Louis, there is no doubt that she would not have been able to live in Florida for a couple years and in London for six years otherwise. But then that is what happens in marriage, two people pool their hopes and resources together. It is also overlooked that Prince Louis benefited too, by the unrecognized household labour of a 'trailing spouse' (Wilcox, 2014).

At the Florida Institute of Technology, her husband had studied aviation and obtained his private pilot licence – it follows that where

Louis went, naturally so did his wife, Tessy, and their two sons. It is good business for any organization posting an employee to an overseas assignment to make provisions for the entire family. Stinting on relocation expenses and support for family would potentially doom the posting's success. Many international schools, colleges, and universities enroll students whose tuition costs are paid for by company budgets or the military or the US Office of Overseas Schools and Department of Defense Education Activity.

Many trailing spouses put their own careers, education, and extended family lives on hold due to the circumstances of the overseas post and an enlightened organization will make spousal benefits part of total compensation package. An enlightened monarchy does the same. In 2003, Mette-Marit, the new crown princess of Norway, relocated with her husband to London for his studies at the London School of Economics and Political Science (Royal House of Norway, 2017). She took courses at SOAS, University of London. (Royal House of Norway, 2017) It is unfair to judge Tessy differently from Mette-Marit.

There is nothing out of the ordinary that Princess Tessy also enrolled in university studies when Prince Louis relocated to the UK to study at Richmond, the American University in London, from 2010 to 2014. Choosing the same university as her husband was not a stretch as Richmond has a fine reputation, the couple is familiar with the American system from their time in Florida, and it probably made sense logistically for child care.

Juggling domestic responsibilities, course assignments, and charity work is what mothers do and Tessy had to combine all these with occasional appearances at royal events in Luxembourg before graduating at age 29 in 2014 with her bachelor's in international relations (Salens, Louis et Tessy de Luxembourg : diplômés de l'université à Londres, 2014). Tessy doing it all again in pursuit of a more challenging master's degree at SOAS, University of London, is at odds of the image of a gold digging trophy wife.

Another important point, a gold digger usually does not divorce. As per this classic I Love Lucy episode, The Black Wig (IMDb.com, 2018), the received wisdom is to stick to him like glue:

> **Ethel Mertz**: [*Lucy is furious that Ricky flirted with her in a black Italian-cut wig, pretending not to know her*] It's a terrible thing to say about anybody, but I guess Ricky's just a man.
> **Lucy Ricardo**: Yeah, well, I'll get even with him.
> **Ethel Mertz**: What are you gonna do?
> **Lucy Ricardo**: I'll leave him. No, that's probably what he wants.
> **Ethel Mertz**: Yeah, stay married to him. That'll teach him!

A trophy wife is an habituée of London Fashion Week and the reality show circuit. Princess Tessy has a fulltime job and works and makes appearances for various charities, so she hardly fits the 'gold digger' label that tabloids fling about. With the United Kingdom exiting the European Union on March 29 2019, like most Europeans citizens ahead of Brexit (De Peyer, 2018), Tessy is rightly proactive in taking action to regularize the family finances in their London home base.

C. *Meghan Markle: Con Te Partiro*

Elizabeth II gave Prince Harry and Meghan the best wedding gift on April 16, 2018 when Kensington Palace tweeted her appointment of him as Commonwealth Youth Ambassador. At age 33, his job "…will see Prince Harry work to create links between young people and leaders and help them address social, environmental and economic challenges around the world." (news.com.au, 2018)

Adding this to his Invictus Games roving ambassador role, the first years of the couple's marriage will be spent travelling the world. In my opinion, that wedding gift gives this couple the best chance to make their marriage one of lasting happiness. Some observers say it is insufficient given the degree of sacrifice Meghan Markle has made – giving up her acting career and independence. But in my opinion, her shelf life as an actress in demand was getting short anyways. Even in light of the #MeToo, TV and movie roles for women beyond her thirties are scarce. Unless you are a Shakespearean-trained Judi Dench or Meryl Streep, the entertainment industry does not have much camera time for women of a certain age (Lang & Holmes, 2017). Most women actors eventually segue into teaching, mentoring, talent agent, directing, documentaries, producing or other behind-the-scenes roles or create roles for themselves like Project Runway or American Idol or Real Housewives of Beverly Hills.

Steve Hewlett's documentary, Reinventing the Royals, puts into context Prince Harry's vociferous response to the leaking of her romance with Meghan Markle in November 2017. Harry seems to have accepted that his role as a prince means media attention and a platform for his causes but he insists on a personal life that he can conduct in privacy:

> "William and Harry appear to be entirely relaxed in a multimedia age," he explains. "They are better adapted to it than their predecessors. They are relaxed. They get it. On the other hand, they are somewhat more reserved about it.
>
> "They accept public duties and the need to have a public presence. But they want a private life that's completely private. In the era of social media, the internet, smartphones with cameras, the old rules are up the creek. **(BBC, 2015)**

For the first time since she graduated from Northwestern University, Meghan will take on true diplomatic responsibilities. Once she marries Harry, the two will be the UK's international glam couple (Duboff, 2018). The new Duke and Duchess of Sussex are reminiscent of the 1930s Prince George, Duke of Kent, and his duchess, HRH Princess

Marina of Greece, both eye-catching star quality (National Portrait Gallery UK, 2018). The new Duchess of Sussex's wedding gown could be seen a diplomatic nod to that worn in 2000 by Panamanian-American designer Angela Brown, when she married HSH Prince Maximillian of Liechtenstein (Paras, 2018). With a bateau neck and three-quarter sleeves, Princess Angela designed the gown herself.

Being intelligent and an Enneagram 7 Promoter Self-Preservation subtype, she will willingly undergo training in royal protocol in the Inner Process quadrant under the supervision of a Prince Harry who does not appear to take it all too seriously himself. As the second son and now sixth in line, and a reservoir of public goodwill, the new Duke of Sussex gets away a more lighthearted style of executive coaching.

It seems that the announcement of Harry's appointment is not a big surprise. In the engagement interview, Meghan had spoken about travelling the Commonwealth.

> MARKLE: "I'm excited to really just get to know more about the different communities here, the smaller organizations who are working on the same causes that I have always been passionate about under this umbrella, and also being able to go around to the Commonwealth." (Reilly, 2017)

As Andrew Morton points out, "She will have grasped instantly that here we have a situation where she's giving up a lot in order to hopefully achieve a lot more. She's exchanged her megaphone … for the world wide web and for international influence and ongoing influence." (Craw, 2018) Stamping her Commonwealth priority right from the beginning, the national flowers of each of the 53 members is sewn into her wedding veil attached to her Clare Waight Keller-designed Givenchy gown (Lam, 2018)

Meghan does not even have to toe the party line of the UK government. She could be forgiven for being outspoken because she and Harry are Commonwealth ambassadors, not British diplomats. The UK Foreign service diplomatic corps have to stay 'on message'; Commonwealth Youth Ambassadors have no such restriction. That's a handy cover for freedom of expression, that suits Enneagram 7 Promoter Princess just fine.

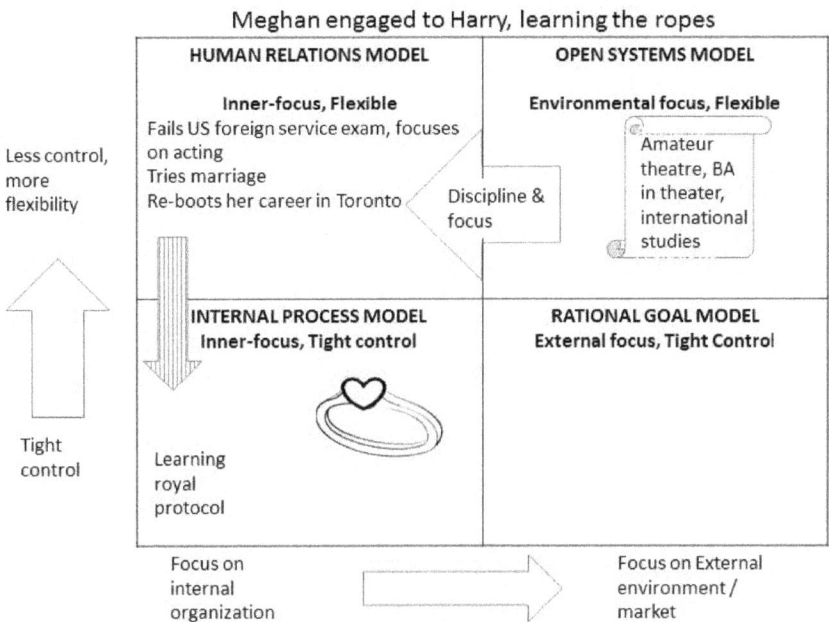

As Harry said about his Youth Ambassador role, "...my job will be to listen to you, my duty will be to ensure that your ideas, concerns, thoughts and hopes are heard," (James, 2017) That said, this is not the most onerous type of job, most of which come with strict targets and measurable outcomes. Listening tours have their usefulness (Lashinsky, 2017). But they should be prepared for an earful.

They can go 'off message and off road' because their ostensible mission is to listen. So mark my words, if and when certain Commonwealth countries, and certain politicians like Ann Widdecomb (Oppenheim, 2018) disapprove of their support of LGBT, Harry and Meghan can deflect by saying they echo the opinions of young people, no disrespect intended. In this, they have the example of the Prince of Wales, whose opinions on a variety of topics in well-known. (Radio Times, 2015)

The Commonwealth comprises 53 countries, 19 of which are in Africa. Harry has often spoken of leaving the UK and living in Africa and Elizabeth II has given into his wish. The Youth Ambassador role is his chance to officially minimize the time spent in England.

> "They're going to lead a much looser life than William and Catherine because of the international dimension of their royal duties. Harry has just been made an Ambassador for the Commonwealth – and he's often spoken about not wanting to live in England and about seeing Africa as his second home." (Morton, The things I've learnt about Meghan Markle, by her unofficial royal biographer, 2018)

The Commonwealth Youth Ambassador media attention may have real spinoff benefits economically and promote tourism.

> Eliza Anyangwe, **the founder of The Nzinga Effect**, a platform that tells African women's stories, said the royals appear to be drawn to a certain image of the continent.
>
> "The Africa they see -- and I believe love -- is the Africa of a National Geographic: stunning landscapes and peculiar cultures," she said.
>
> "The great travesty about Africa for a lot of white people is that it happens to be populated by Africans. So they seek after the wilderness or the parts most reminiscent of Europe -- such as Cape Town (South Africa) for example,"
>
> Louise Nyamu-Steinbeck, a political scientist in the Kenyan capital, Nairobi.
>
> Since colonial history cannot be changed or erased, Nyamu-Steinbeck said, African nations should look at the big picture and utilize the relationship to boost tourism, which is a big part of their economies.

"The biggest reward this attention could accord Africa is for those beyond her borders to understand that the continent is so much more than orphans, famine, disaster, poverty and corruption -- that it offers a well-trained service industry, a sizable educated elite, and technological innovations galore," (Karimi, 2017)

7. Enneagram for Happily Ever After

When it comes to living Happily Ever After, it all depends on her taking care of herself and doing the inner work – I suggest anyone aware of Enneagram type to consider the very effective strategies that Lynn Roulo offers in *Headstart for Happiness: Enneagram and Kundalini* and her videos and workshops - and the organizational culture of The Firm at the moment she invests herself in. Above all, the degree of self awareness and inner work in grounded reality is where she stands with or without The Firm.

A case in point is [Grace, Princess of Monaco](). The first jet-age princess from America, blonde Oscar-winning actress Grace Kelly, from a prosperous Irish Catholic family in the construction industry (the Philadelphia version of the Trumps), at 26 she landed 'the best role of her life', guffawed iconic director Sir Alfred Hitchcock. (Spoto, 2009)

But post-wedding, Donald Spoto goes on to largely (albeit, sadly) refute this. Grace Kelly did her work as Princess of Monaco spectacularly, a consort to Prince Rainier that brought a true 'breath of fresh air' to the country. The court may have initially been suspicious, resentful, and resistant to her attempts to update the way things are done but the Monegasque people liked her. Somerset Maugham pithy description of 'Monte Carlo is a sunny place for shady people' took Grace's elegance and kindness to give the principality a 'make-over' and a 'reset' of its place in Europe. Few foreign royals attended her wedding, at her funeral 26 years later, everyone came to honor her.

To this day, she is missed by her family and her country.

But right to the end, what Grace missed from her bachelorette life was the acting fraternity. It was her métier to act on stage in <u>the company of other professional actors</u>. As an actor amongst actors, she hugely enjoyed the camaraderie of the set. The fourth film with Hitchcock never happened and she had to make do with poetry readings, serving on the board of Twentieth Century Fox, and occasional appearances for marketing purposes. Still, these hardly need a mastery of the craft of acting.

Andrew Morton says, "…(B)eing royal is a bit like acting. You're on stage for a period of time, and then you take the makeup off, and off you go home." (Davies, 2018). As wife of the Sovereign Prince of Monaco, however, Grace did not have much that respite. Neither does her son's wife, Princess Charlene. But Meghan Markle and Princess Tessy and Sarah Ferguson were not married to the sovereign, their prince were not even on the podium of the succession Olympics so they can pick and choose the degree to which they are in the spotlight.

Also, the royal household HR have slowly been updating what a princess can actually humanly handle. Until the death of Diana, Princess of Wales, newcomers were expected to handle an inordinately large number of charities. Diana herself was patron of over 100 until 1996 (BBC, 2018). She then chose to focus on fewer than a dozen after her divorce became final. (BBC, 2018) This more selective approach to charities that correspond more to her personal interests as well as to devote more attention to them is what the Duke and Duchess of Cambridge have done. Not a figurehead but a patron who is more engaged is the new model.

However, it does require more princesses-on-the-payroll, an arithmetic that is at odds with the Prince of Wales's preference to slim down the monarchy. In being squeezed for personnel, he may have to seriously consider taking on board the other blood royal princesses, the York sisters. Once Eugenie is married to Jack Brooksbank, and is more settled, Prince Charles may feel the specter of ex sister-in-law Sarah Ferguson is less daunting.

As Enneagram 7 Promoter Princess and the ease to which she can let things go will stand them in good stead. Meghan speaks directly to this in her engagement interview, indicating that she is not personally invested to the extent that Grace had been in 'actress' or 'stage career' identify. (Yes, it must be reiterated again that Grace Kelly's acting talent saw her working with the finest directors and actors in her era – who would not miss working at the top of your game? Once she filmed *Mogambo* and *High Noon*, Grace Kelly was beyond auditioning for roles, and left at the pinnacle of her career.) Very much having chalked up the experience of working in a long-running cable television series, Meghan Markle is transitioning to another form of being in the public eye:

> BBC: But also giving up your career?
>
> Markle: I don't see it as giving anything up. I just see it as a change.
>
> Prince Harry: It is a new challenge.
>
> Markle: It's a new chapter, right? Also keep in mind I had been working on my show for seven years. So we were very, very fortunate to be able to have that sort of longevity on a series. For me, once we hit the 100 episode marker, I thought, you know what, I have ticked this box, and I feel very proud of the work I had done there and now it's time to work as team with

you. Yeah.. (Reilly, 2017)

 The Enneagram 7 Promoter is keenly aware of the magnetic draw of the title of princess. Princess Tessy has said as much in her interview with RTLuxembourg - it helps her advocacy work as long as she has her title. After one has been UN goodwill ambassador and attended banquets and spoken at the UN, you are set for life among the global elite, a glamocracy of sports stars, entertainment pundits, wealthy 1%, politicians. (Mount, 2017).

For the Enneagram 7 Promoter Princess, the spotlight in and of itself is not important but it is the platform for her own opinions. Contrast this to a stage like the [Stratford](#) or [Shaw](#) Festivals or The Globe Theatre, where she is expected to speak the words of Shakespeare, to know her lines, with no deviation from the script. The platform can be improv; not a tightly scripted delivery to an audience. Etiquette expert Liz Brewer offers:

> "She needs to remember now that she is no longer an actress acting a part - although she is a very good actress. She is now part of 'Brand Britain', and as such, everything she is doing will be geared towards that." (Mills, 2018)

The new Duchess of Sussex can free style and parkour in the interest of getting the crowd on side within the Rational Goal quadrant. Only she does not come off as a hypocrite lecturing the poor and disenfranchised from the palace perch - and this advice from Piers Morgan who has always been in her camp (Morgan, 2018).

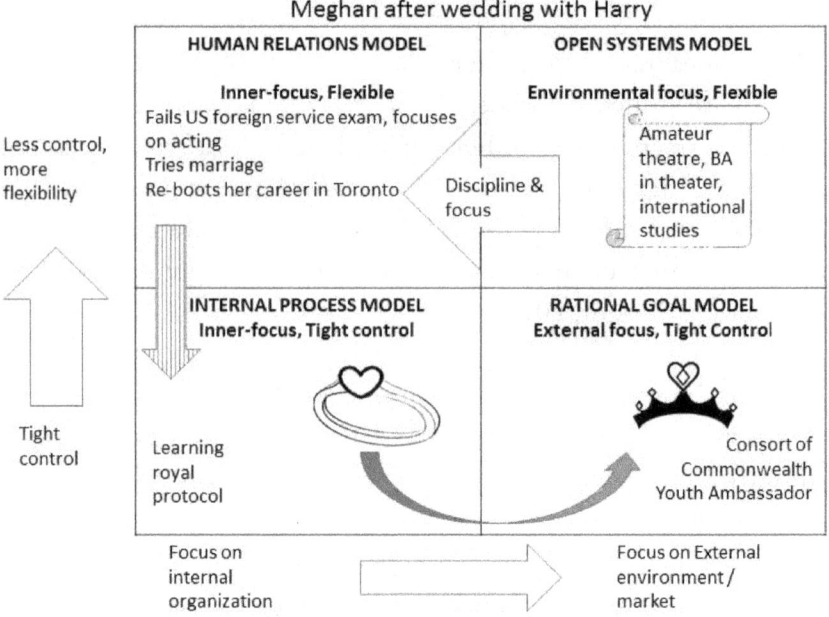

With the Prince of Wales escorting his younger son's bride to the altar (Millar, 2018, Meghan Markle is leaving all the Markles and their crab syndrome drama (Weiji, 2016) in her past and shut that door. The footage of the wedding shows no Markle members inside St George's chapel, no one else from her mother's side either, just the carefully-chosen set representing the network of the Enneagram 7 Promoter princess Self-Preservation subtype. With the only blood relative present being her mother, it makes a statement of who has a place in her future. She is fully embracing a royal life as HRH the Duchess of Sussex with its traditions, limits, opportunities, family, and Harry.

That is all well and good if the Duke and Duchess of Sussex stay married. But what if they end up divorcing? There is the shadow side of marrying royals - once one is in, she relinquishes a normal ordinary private life. That door swings shut. As The Eagles put it, "You can check out anytime you like but you can never leave…" In the Japanese imperial family, the Imperial Household has control over the new princess's every move, according to author Ben Hills in his biography of Masako Owada, now [Crown Princess of Japan](#) (Kato, 2009)

Widowed former First Lady Jacqueline Kennedy eloquently summed up the dilemma in this response: "When her friend Truman Capote asked her why she became Mrs. Onassis, she said, "I can't very well marry a dentist from New Jersey!" (Cassidy, 2012)

Jade Jodelle, in her YouTube video excoriating the lack of social mobility in England, points out that the charities are often well-intentioned but often hire only decision-makers who are the same upper class, (Joddle, 2015) which only reinforces England's social mobility problem (Milburn, 2017).

With that being the case, if Enneagram 7 Promoters who are now ex-princesses could be cast adrift, unemployable, struck off of invitation lists, their talents to make a better world would lie fallow.

The way back from 'social Siberia' for the Enneagram 7 Promoter is, ironically, not through her tried-and-tired public appearances, external validation and total flexibility of her default happy space of the Open Systems quadrant. Rather, it is through the unseen focus and discipline of the Human Relations Model quadrant. For Sarah Ferguson, it is the fruit of years of behind-closed-door nurturing of her two daughters. People tend to say that Princesses Beatrice and Eugenie are genuinely nice women who have emerged from their parents's divorce relatively well adjusted (Finn, 2018). Penny Junor is certain that Harry and Meghan invited Sarah to the wedding , although no longer married to Andrew, because she remains his York cousins's mother :

> "Harry is very close to Eugenie and Beatrice, closer, I think, than William. Harry really is a friend. And while Fergie may have exhibited poor judgement over the years, and got herself into terrible messes, Harry would absolutely see that she is a nice woman who found being in the Royal Family extremely

difficult. She made mistakes and caused embarrassment, but God knows Harry has too. Harry is a very tolerant bloke, the kind to let bygones be bygones rather than hold grudges." (Sykes, The Rehabilitation of Fergie, the Comeback Duchess, 2018)

Unlike Prince William and Prince Harry, even Sarah and her sister Jane, the York princesses were not deprived of their mother as they grew up. Although Major Ron Ferguson did what he could to bring up Sarah and older sister Jane in their teen years. (Vickers, 2003), research has shown that the same-gender parent has a crucial role in adolescent development (Pickhardt, 2010). Susan Wright Ferguson abandoned her daughters in their crucial teenage years to set up home in Argentina with her new husband, and the girls suffered. When it was her turn to divorce, Sarah adamantly refused to follow her mother's example. Because Andrew continued his naval career and was hardly around, it was Sarah Ferguson Duchess of York's choice to step up to the responsible parent role: "the only thing I know I've done 100 percent right is be a good mother." (Sales, 2011)

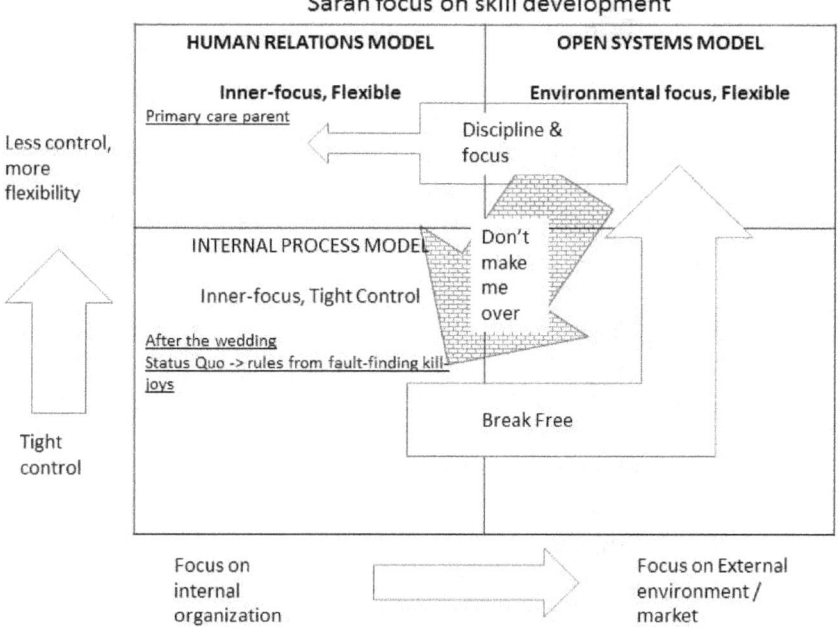

Sarah was indeed invited to Harry and Meghan's wedding:
https://www.telegraph.co.uk/content/dam/fashion/2018/05/19/TELEMMGLP
ICT000164007703_trans_NvBQzQNjv4BqqTYIvvm7YQR0p3S9ocyDykii1AgTZ
sMMTT0wSlVdyEs.jpeg?imwidth=1400

It is not a coincidence that Tessy Antony went the same route – this is the Enneagram 7 Promoter's path to self-awareness. Similarly, London-based Princess Tessy is the primary care parent for her two sons who are at school in England. (Their father Prince Louis is based in Paris, according to reports from the Grand Ducal official visit to France in 2017.) The reason why Tessy has her act together at the young age of 32 is because she deliberately shifted from the Open Systems quadrant to the Human Relations quadrant earlier, at the age of 20!

Making the best of that reality is what the Enneagram 7 Promoter Princess can do very well. Accepting what is present and bringing optimism to the platform they are landed with from a home space of grounded reality. In the words of Sarah Ferguson on CNN with Piers Morgan:

> PIERS MORGAN: Do you ever -- I mean, putting Prince Andrew to one side, do you ever wonder what your life would have been like if you just met an ordinary guy who wasn't a royal or wasn't famous, and could have had just a very nice anonymous life?
>
> FERGUSON: You know, Dr. Phil said, "Sarah, why don't you go and live in Australia with your sister and go quiet? I said, oh, no, I don't think I can manage that. (LAUGHTER)
>
> FERGUSON: I don't think I'm that sort of person. I think I'm just I'm always wanting to do more. I want to use my life. I want to -- especially now that I've changed this course of health and wellness and getting creative and really using it the right way. It's pretty exciting.
>
> So, I don't think I would have ever gone to live in Gloucester with (INAUDIBLE), no. ..." (CNN.com, 2011)

In short, this is Sarah Ferguson being as focused as an Enneagram 7 Promoter Princess as she could potentially be. She is right about not managing a quiet life far away in Australia. Sarah Ferguson is not going quietly away to Obscurity Corners with her tail between her legs. However, what is receding is the hankering for the spotlight, the 3 Fs ([FOMO, FOBLO, FOGKO](#)) (Rudulph, 2017). She has moved on, in realizing in wisdom that she has 'been there, done that'. Coming to that grounded reality, she is in the pole position of dictating the terms of which she engages the media, usually social media of Instagram, with the expressed intention to use the platform to further her charity, Children in Crisis.

After all these years, she and Andrew finally have themselves a house they are content in. Albeit their jointly-owned home is located outside of the UK, in Switzerland (English, Doyle, & Martin, Prince Andrew buys £13million ski lodge: Never mind the sex slave scandal - Prince and Fergie snap up snow palace, 2015) - which makes sense as property in England gets more expensive and the Yorks moves to the periphery of the royal family.

Rumour has it that the Prince of Wales, in anticipation of his reign, is already slimming down the royal family to a core of four: Her Majesty, the Prince of Wales, his two sons, and their spouses, as per the Diamond Jubilee celebrations in 2012 (Kay & Levy, Princes at war: How Charles' plans for a slimmed-down monarchy have 'driven a dagger through Andrew's heart' - and sparked a Palace power struggle, 2012). The collateral royals, his siblings and cousins are publicly moved out of the inner circle. Shorn of his trade ambassador role, Andrew with Sarah see themselves spending more time outside of the UK, perhaps together. After all these years, she finally has her man the way it was originally envisioned.

> "…we are the happiest divorced couple. We are happy the way things are. . . . We don't have to get married again in order to live happily ever after." (Jordan, 2009)

By shifting to a grounded reality in the Rational Goal quadrant, Sarah Ferguson does not have to be front and centre. That part of her life is over, not simply because of her divorce but because she accepts it is the turn of the next generation. And instead of being the front man and promoter of other people's causes, she focuses on the charities she herself has founded (Clifton, 2013) and promotes on her Instagram and other social media.

Touchingly, in the chapel, the Duke and the Duchess of York with their two daughters and Eugenie's fiancé, Jack Brooksbank, witnessed the wedding of Harry and Meghan (Vulpo, 2018). In October 2018, when Princess Eugenie marries Jack, it might feel like 1947 all over again, if in an alternate universe Edward VIII had stayed on the throne and the Duke of York walked his daughter down the aisle and the We

Four added a son-in-law. The writer in Sarah might share her sentiments in a letter like George VI's (Schwartz, 2013) .

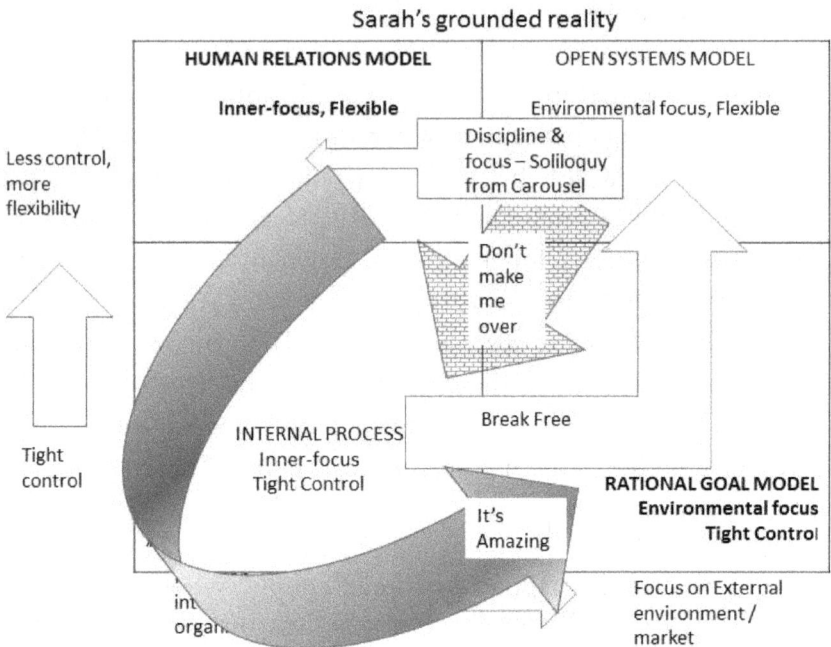

Tessy Antony, Princess of Luxembourg is an Enneagram 7 Promoter of a generation more recent than Sarah Ferguson. At age 32, she has on her CV her service in the army, earned two higher-education degrees, and is on a fulfilling career path. By the time she reaches 36, the Duchess of Sussex's age now, her two sons will be in their late teens, one milestone she shares with the late Diana Princess of Wales (Mellado, 2019).

In her native Luxembourgish , Princess Tessy speaks frankly in a fall 2017 interview from London that "having a title truly opens many doors I want to use this opportunity to do something good – for me it is not about having a title and doing nothing with it…" (RTL.lu, 2017)

Perhaps in preparation for the time in which she no longer has the princess title, her Instagram name is Tessy_from_Luxembourg and her linkedin is Tessy Antony. Her pragmatic approach is reminiscent of an apocryphal story... About 40-some years ago, so the story goes, the Premier of Manitoba, Canada, and his wife were finishing at a public event in the rural part of the province. As they left, they met an old beau of hers, who owned a very small business. Later on, Premier Ed Schreyer kidded his wife, Lily, "Well, what do you think would have happened if you had married him?"

Her reply, "I would have become the wife of the Premier of Manitoba."

Ed Schreyer was later appointed in 1979 by Prime Minister Pierre Trudeau as the Governor General of Canada, the ceremonial head of state, and served very well in that capacity. It was in a large part due to Lily Schreyer and her management of their family of four and her graciousness as the doyenne of Rideau Hall that his term representing Canadians is remembered so fondly (The Governor General of Canada, 2018).

In the circuitous manner, this example speaks to Tessy as a representative, a Promoter in the best sense of the word, not just of herself but of her country, her gender. Her commitment to serving her country predated meeting her husband – an early commitment at the young age of 18 when she joined the army. Her support of women as a UN peacekeeper came about after basic training, serving in Kosovo and commiserating with women victims of war crimes. And in her charity work since 2009 with the added title of Princess of Luxembourg, Tessy promotes global awareness of her country.

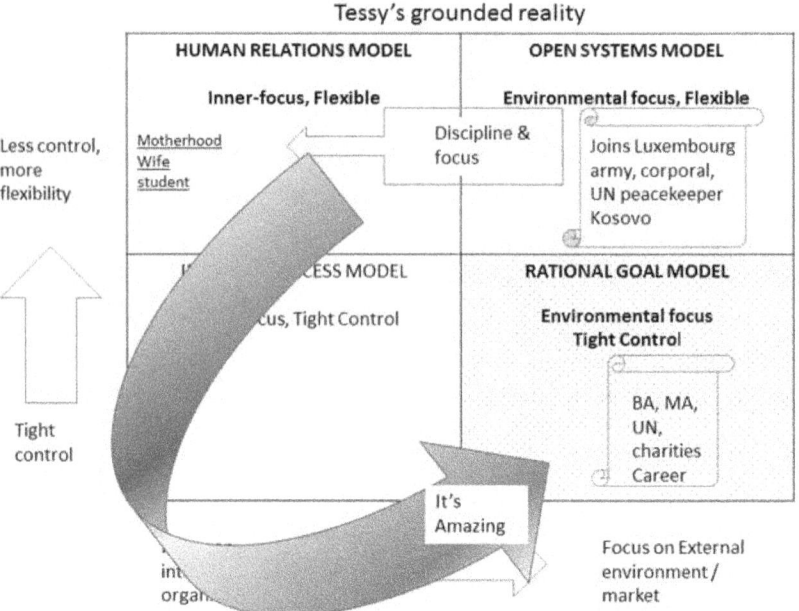

'Even if one day or another I lose my title, that does not change who I am, I am proud to be a Luxembourger." (RTL.be, 2017). Her professional work and her charity work will continue, regardless of her being Tessy of Luxembourg or Tessy from Luxembourg (Weber, 2017). In short, ensconced in the Rational Goal quadant, shorn of the bells and whistles of compulsion, and laser-focused on the future the self-aware Enneagram 7 Promoter channels her talents going forward in those spectacular gladiator stilettos.

When anyone gets out of compulsive behavior through the transformative effects of deliberate attention, you have obtained freedom, as Enneagram teacher Patricia Shreenan affirms (Sister Patricia Shreenan, 2018). The inner work you put in to sorting through negativity and pain unearths your potential - you are meeting yourself for the very first time. When your attention and energy flows to the sweet spot of selfhood, that is dynamic. The soundtrack when you reap the harvest of inner work is Feeling Good (BBC Music,

Royalty Meets Enneagram: Understanding Personality Style 7

2016) https://www.youtube.com/watch?v=HhfPFpAfU_A because to stand on this new grounded reality feels good!

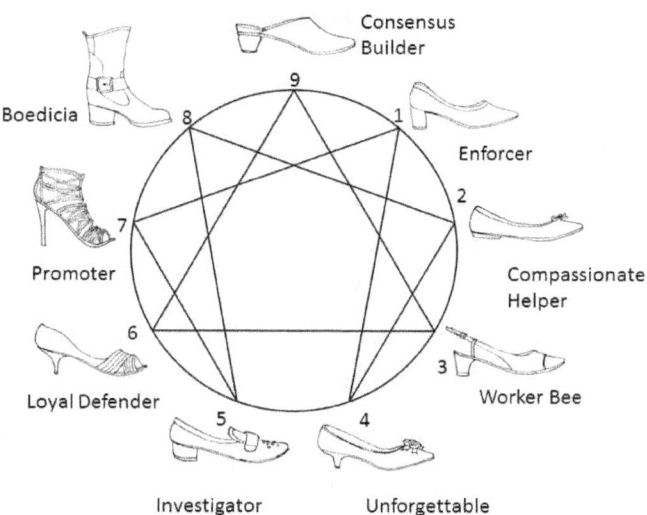

###

REFERENCES IN THE SERIES

Almaas, A. H. (1998). *Facets of Unity, the Enneagram of Holy Ideas*. Berkeley, USA: Diamond Books.

Bain, Neil and Hugh O'Donnell. (2001). *Media, Monarchy & Power: the Postmodern Culture in Europe* (European Studies Series). Bristol: Intellect Books.

Barlett, Carolyn. (2003). *The Enneagram Field Guide: Notes on Using the Enneagram in Counseling, Therapy, and Personal Growth*. Portland, Oregon USA: The Enneagram Consortium.

Bast, Mary and Clarence Thomson. (2005). *Out of the Box: Coaching with the Enneagram*. Louisburg, Kansas: Ninestar Publishing.

Chestnut, Beatrice. (2013). *The Complete Enneagram: 27 Paths to Greater Self Knowledge*. Berkeley, USA: She Writes Press.

Condon, Thomas. (1999). *The Enneagram Movie and Video Guide*. Portland, OR: The Enneagram Consortium.

Daniels, David, & Price, Virginia. (2000). *The Essential Enneagram: The Definitive Personality Test & Self-Discovery Guide*. San Francisco: HarperSanFrancisco.

Goldberg, Michael. (1998). *Getting Your Boss's Number*. New York: Marlow & Co.

Haidt, Jonathan. (2006). *The Happiness Hypothesis: Finding Modern Truth in Ancient Wisdom*. New York: Basic Books.

Hampson, Michael. (2005). *Head versus Heart and Our Gut Reactions: The 21st Century Enneagram*. New York: O Books.

Hartman, Christine. (2008). *Dating the Divorced Man: Sort Through the Baggage to Decide If He's Right for You*. Avon, USA: Adams Media.

Hurley, Kathleen V and Theodorre E. Dobson. (1991). *What's My Type?* San Francisco: Harper San Francisco.

Keyes, Margaret Frings. (1992). *Emotions and the Enneagram: Working Through Your Shadow Life Script*. Muir Beach, USA: Molysdatur Publications.

Lapid-Bogda, Ginger, (2004). *Bringing out the best in yourself at work: How to use the Enneagram system for success*. Toronto: McGraw Hill.

Levine, Janet. (2003). *Knowing Your Parenting Personality*. Hoboken: John Wiley & Sons.

Maitri, Sandra. (2000). *The Spiritual Dimension of the Enneagram*. New York: Putnam.

Naranjo, Claudio. (1994). Character *and Neurosis, an Integrative View*. Nevada City, CA: Gateways/IDHHB, Inc.

Naranjo, Claudio. (1997). *Enneatypes in Psychotherapy*. Prescott, AZ: Holm Press.

Nathans, Hannah. (2003). *The Enneagram at Work: Towards Personal Mastery and Social Intelligence*. The Netherlands: Scriptum Management.

Palmer, Helen. (1988). *The Enneagram: Understanding Yourself and the Others in Your Life*. San Francisco: HarperCollins.

Palmer, Helen & Paul Brown. (1997). *The Enneagram Advantage: Putting the Nine Personality Types to Work in the Office*. New York: Three Rivers Press.

Peñafiel, Jaime (2008). *Juan Carlos y Sofía, Retrato de un matrimonio*. Madrid: La Esfera de los Libros.

Riso, Don and Hudson, Russ. (1999). *The Wisdom of the Enneagram: The Complete Guide to Psychological and Spiritual Growth for the Nine Personality Types*. New York: Bantam.

Rohr, Richard. (1997). *Discovering the Enneagram*. New York: Crossroads Publishing Company.

Rose, Colin and Nicholl, Malcolm. (1996). *Accelerated Learning for the 21st Century*. London: Piatkus.

Roulo, Lynn. (2016). *Headstart for Happiness: A Guide Book Using Kundalini Yoga and the Enneagram*. San Francisco: Rasayan Center, LLC

Searle, Judith. (2001). *The Literary Enneagram, Characters from the Inside Out*. Portland, OR: The Enneagram Consortium.

Thomson, Clarence and Condon, Thomas. (2001). *Enneagram Applications: Personality Styles in Business, Therapy, Spirituality, and Daily Life*. Portland, OR: The Enneagram Consortium.

Villemann, Trine. (2008). *1015 Copenhagen K: Mary's Dysfunctional In-Laws*. Brunham,

UK: Andartes Press.

Wagele, Elizabeth, and Baron, Renee. (1995). *Are You My Type, Am I Yours?* San Francisco: HarperSanFrancisco.

Wagele, Elizabeth, and Baron, Renee. (1994). *The Enneagram Made Easy*. San Francisco: HarperSanFrancisco.

Wagele, Elizabeth. (1997). *The Enneagram of Parenting*. New York: Harper Collins.

Wagner, Jerome P. (1996). *The Enneagram Spectrum of Personality Styles: An Introductory Guide*. Portland, OR: Metamorphous Press.

Webb, Karen A. (2013). *Principles of The Enneagram, 2nd edition*. London: Singing Dragon.

Zuercher, Suzanne. (1992). *Enneagram Spirituality*. Notre Dame, IN USA: Ave Maria Press.

References in Enneagram 7 Promoter Princess

[2017] EWHC 3095 (Fam), ZC16D00198 (Royal Courts of Justice UK 12 5, 2017).

1 Hare Court. (2018, April 21). *Deborah Bangay QC.* Retrieved from 1 Hare Court: https://www.1hc.com/people/deborah-bangay-qc/

Aanmoen, O. (2018, March 28). *Margareta, Custodian of the Crown of Romania addresses Parliament following major demonstrations.* Retrieved from Royal Central: http://royalcentral.co.uk/europe/romania/margareta-custodian-of-the-crown-of-romania-addresses-parliament-following-major-demonstrations-99174

Ahmed, K. (1996, November 9). *Sex, lies and tales of royalty.* Retrieved from The Irish Times: https://www.irishtimes.com/news/sex-lies-and-tales-of-royalty-1.104501

Andrews, M. (2018, May 16). *RIGHT ROYAL MESS How the Palace's failure to look after an overwhelmed Thomas Markle has left poor Meghan devastated just days before she marries Harry.* Retrieved from The Sun: https://www.thesun.co.uk/news/6296441/meghan-markle-tough-relationship-with-dad-thomas/

AOL.com editors. (2017, August 17). *Prince William is breaking royal protocol by flying with his kids.* Retrieved from AOL.com: https://www.aol.com/article/lifestyle/2017/08/17/prince-william-breaks-royal-protocol-by-flying-with-kids/23080737/

Apple Inc. (2018, May 18). *Jonathan Ive, Chief Design Officer - Apple Leadership.* Retrieved from Apple Inc: https://www.apple.com/ca/leadership/jonathan-ive/

Armecin, C. (2018, April 13). *Meghan Markle 'Very Careful About Brand*

Meghan,' Andrew Morton Says*. Retrieved from International Business Times: http://www.ibtimes.com/meghan-markle-very-careful-about-brand-meghan-andrew-morton-says-2671608

Armée luxembourgeoise. (2018, April 10). *Grades*. Retrieved from Armée luxembourgeoise: http://www.armee.lu/organisation/personnel/grades

Associated Press. (2007, April 11). *Prof has advice for tackling workplace jerks. Is your boss a screamer or a demeane? The best solution: just quit*. Retrieved from NBC News: http://www.nbcnews.com/id/17629928/

Australia, 6. M. (2018, April 15). *Royal Fairytale | 60 Minutes Australia*. Retrieved from YouTube: https://www.youtube.com/watch?v=zgWflTivgk4

Barger, B. (2018, May 16). *EXCLUSIVE: Tessy Antony, Princess of Luxembourg talks charity work*. Retrieved from Royal Central: http://royalcentral.co.uk/europe/luxembourg/exclusive-tessy-antony-princess-of-luxembourg-talks-charity-work-102290

Barger, B. (2018, May 13). *EXCLUSIVE: Tessy Antony, Princess of Luxembourg talks life, education, social media in two part interview*. Retrieved from Royal Central: http://royalcentral.co.uk/europe/luxembourg/exclusive-tessy-antony-princess-of-luxembourg-talks-life-and-education-in-two-part-interview-102226

Barrett, K. (2010, January 11). *How Deep is Your Bench?* Retrieved from Organization Impact: http://www.organizationimpact.com/how-deep-is-your-bench/

Barrowclough, A. (2009, March 9). *Knights and Dames titles to return to New Zealand*. Retrieved from The Times of London: http://www.timesonline.co.uk/tol/news/world/article5866547.ece

BBC. (1998, January 28). *Cookbook author Fergie admits: 'I can't cook'*. Retrieved from BBC: http://news.bbc.co.uk/2/hi/51275.stm

BBC. (2015, February 19). *First family versus fourth estate: the new royal rules*. Retrieved from BBC: http://www.bbc.com/news/uk-31506822

BBC. (2018, May 4). *Diana Charity List - ceased to be involved with in 1996*. Retrieved from BBC Diana: In Memoriam: http://www.bbc.co.uk/news/special/politics97/diana/charlist.html

BBC. (2018, May 4). *Diana charity list after divorce*. Retrieved from BBC Diana: In Memoriam: http://www.bbc.co.uk/news/special/politics97/diana/dichar2.html

BBC Music. (2016, November 3). *Bublé at the BBC: Michael transforms into sales assistant Dion*. Retrieved from YouTube: https://www.youtube.com/watch?v=I-yfuM_QDcQ

Borrill, R. (1996, October 12). *Tabloid treatment turns trouble at palace into "Dallas*. Retrieved from The Irish Times: https://www.irishtimes.com/culture/tabloid-treatment-turns-trouble-at-palace-into-dallas-1.94985

Boy Scout Trail. (2018, April 25). *Stay On the Sunny Side Song*. Retrieved from Boy Scout Trail: http://www.boyscouttrail.com/content/song/stay_on_the_sunny_side-1130.asp

Boycott, R. (1996, November 17). *Scenes from a jolly awkward life*. Retrieved from The Independent : https://www.independent.co.uk/arts-entertainment/scenes-from-a-jolly-awkward-life-1352754.html

Brannigan, M. (2018, May 1). *Meghan Markle on the Struggles of*

Getting Into the TV Industry. Retrieved from Marie Claire: https://www.marieclaire.com/celebrity/news/a7733/meghan-markle-interview/

Brown, C. (2018, May 1). *Can This Marriage Be Saved? A real actor joins the longest-running soap opera in history.* Retrieved from The Cut: https://www.thecut.com/2018/05/are-prince-harry-and-meghan-markle-doomed.html

Brown, T. (2010, May 26). *Fergie may be nuts, but she'd have never embarrassed the royals like this if they'd been less stingy.* Retrieved from Daily Mail: http://www.dailymail.co.uk/femail/article-1281446/Sarah-Ferguson-nuts-royals-stingy.html#ixzz5DXnqKewf

Burke, J. (2009, December 13). *Sarah Ferguson produces, and protects, 'The Young Victoria'.* Retrieved from Los Angeles Times: http://articles.latimes.com/2009/dec/13/entertainment/la-ca-fergie13-2009dec13

Byrnes, S. (2005, March 29). *Mark Bolland: Marital aide.* Retrieved from The Independent: https://www.independent.co.uk/news/people/profiles/mark-bolland-marital-aide-530391.html

Carteedge, J. (2008, September 5). *Jane Cartledge: Kids power their way into future.* Retrieved from Daily Star UK: https://www.thestar.co.uk/news/jane-cartledge-kids-power-their-way-into-future-1-253508

Cassidy, T. (2012, May 10). *Has the trophy wife faded into history?* Retrieved from The Boston Globe: https://www.bostonglobe.com/lifestyle/style/2012/05/09/has-trophy-wife-faded-into-history/jkaL96LBahS1aewcOxo2GP/story.html

Cavendish, L. (2009, March 1). *Sarah, Duchess of York exclusive: The only thing I ever succeeded at was failure*. Retrieved from Sunday Telegraph: http://www.telegraph.co.uk/news/newstopics/theroyalfamily/4864811/Sarah-Duchess-of-York-exclusive-The-only-thing-I-ever-succeeded-at-was-failure.html

Chestnut, B. (2010, November 10). *Enneagram Theory: The 'State of the Art' of Enneagram Subtypes*. Retrieved from The Enneagram in Business: http://theenneagraminbusiness.com/subtypes/enneagram-theory-the-state-of-the-art-of-enneagram-subtypes/

Churcher, S. (2011, July 30). *My mother didn't beat me - it was just a joke says Fergie as she backtracks on abuse claims*. Retrieved from Daily Mail: http://www.dailymail.co.uk/news/article-2020672/Sarah-Ferguson-My-mother-didnt-beat--just-joke.html

Clarke-Billings, L. (2018, April 8). *The ruthless side of Meghan Markle: Former agent claims princess-to-be can be 'picky and likes to move on'*. Retrieved from Daily Mirror: https://www.mirror.co.uk/news/uk-news/meghan-markle-is-ruthless-instantly-12328565

Clifton, J. (2013, March 17). *Duchess of York: These children give me hope and faith*. Retrieved from Daily Express: https://www.express.co.uk/news/royal/384780/Duchess-of-York-These-children-give-me-hope-and-faith

CNN.com. (2011, June 11). *transcript - Piers Morgan Tonight - Interview with Sarah Ferguson*. Retrieved from Transcripts CNN.com: http://transcripts.cnn.com/TRANSCRIPTS/1106/12/pmt.01.html

Cohen, H. (2017, December 30). *A new kind of Knight Fever for Miami Beach's Barry Gibb. Is neighbor Phil Collins next?* Retrieved from Miami Herald: http://www.miamiherald.com/entertainment/article192287164.html

Collins, S. T. (2018, March 1). *The 10 Best (and Worst) Best Song Oscar-Winners of All Time*. Retrieved from Rolling Stone: https://www.rollingstone.com/movies/lists/the-10-best-and-worst-best-song-oscar-winners-of-all-time-w517194/best-raindrops-keep-fallin-on-my-head-butch-cassidy-and-the-sundance-kid-1969-w517248

Cooper, A. F. (2007). *Celebrity Diplomacy.* Boulder, USA: Paradigm Publishers/UBC Press.

Craw, V. (2018, April 12). *Meghan Markle described as 'supreme networker' by royal biographer Andrew Morton in new book*. Retrieved from News.com.au: http://www.news.com.au/entertainment/celebrity-life/royals/meghan-markle-described-as-supreme-networker-by-royal-biographer-andrew-morton-in-new-book/news-story/c9d7cd767bfdcec059804607129898d3

Csikszentmihalyi, M. (1998). *Finding Flow: The Psychology Of Engagement With Everyday Life.* New York: Basic Books.

Daily Mail. (2011, June 5). *Fergie breaks down on television and reveals: 'My mother told me I had the devil in me'*. Retrieved from Daily Mail: http://www.dailymail.co.uk/tvshowbiz/article-1394550/Sarah-Ferguson-reveals-television-abuse-inflicted-mother.html

Davies, C. (2018, April 13). *'Team Meghan' helps Markle prepare for life as a princess*. Retrieved from The Guardian: https://www.theguardian.com/uk-news/2018/apr/13/team-meghan-helps-markle-prepare-life-princess

De Peyer, R. (2018, March 29). *'It's terrifying': How 'Brexit day' is leaving London's EU nationals fearing for their futures*. Retrieved from The Evening Standard: https://www.standard.co.uk/news/politics/it-s-terrifying-how-brexit-day-is-leaving-london-s-eu-nationals-fearing-for-their-futures-a3797731.html

Deschamps, T. (. (2018, April 27). *Canadian designers get boost from Meghan Markle's style*. Retrieved from CTV News: https://toronto.ctvnews.ca/canadian-designers-get-boost-from-meghan-markle-s-style-1.3905808

DeYoung, K. (1986, March 20). *At Last Sarah Gets The Ring*. Retrieved from The Washington Post: https://www.washingtonpost.com/archive/lifestyle/1986/03/20/at-last-sarah-gets-the-ring/4aad0bd5-aaad-4c37-ba54-5a626d4f7b46/?utm_term=.cc6441797763

Douglas, W. (2018, May 2). *A complete guide to wedding etiquette – for brides, grooms and guests*. Retrieved from Daily Telegraph: https://www.telegraph.co.uk/weddings/advice/complete-guide-wedding-etiquette-brides-grooms-guests/

Duboff, J. (2018, May 17). *After the Royal Wedding, What's Next for Meghan Markle?* Retrieved from Vanity Fair: https://www.vanityfair.com/style/2018/05/meghan-markle-new-role-life-after-wedding

Duncan, A. (2018, February 13). *What did Meghan Markle's first wedding dress look like for Jamaican wedding to Trevor Engelson?* Retrieved from Metro UK: http://metro.co.uk/2018/02/13/meghan-markles-first-wedding-dress-look-like-happened-jamaican-wedding-trevor-engelson-7309694/

Eade, P. (2017). *Young Prince Philip*. London: Harper Press.

Effervescence Media, G. (2018, January 5). *A Peek Inside Meghan Markle's Shoe Closet: Carolinna Espinosa Sari Gladiator Sandal*. Retrieved from Meghan's Mirror: http://meghansmirror.com/product/meghan-markle-gladiator-sandal/

Embury-Dennis, T. (2018, March 15). *Prince Harry and Meghan Markle wedding should receive no taxpayer money, thousands demand in petition*. Retrieved from The Independent: https://www.independent.co.uk/royalwedding/prince-harry-meghan-markle-royal-wedding-petition-taxpayer-money-public-funding-a8257126.html

English, R. (2011, July 26). *Blubbing Fergie hits a new low: Duchess allows Beatrice and Eugenie to be filmed clearly in distress for latest TV series*. Retrieved from Daily Mail: http://www.dailymail.co.uk/tvshowbiz/article-2018763/Fergie-hits-new-low-Princess-Beatrice-Eugenie-filmed-distress-TV-show.html

English, R., Doyle, J. D., & Martin, A. (2015, January 10). *Prince Andrew buys £13million ski lodge: Never mind the sex slave scandal - Prince and Fergie snap up snow palace*. Retrieved from Daily Mail: http://www.dailymail.co.uk/news/article-2904085/Andrew-buys-13m-ski-lodge-Never-mind-sex-slave-scandal-Prince-Fergie-snap-snow-palace.html

Female First. (2017, February 8). *Dickie Arbiter: Princess Diana was 'a breath of fresh air'*. Retrieved from Female First: http://www.femalefirst.co.uk/royal_family/dickie-arbiter-princess-diana-breath-fresh-air-1033254.html

Ferguson Mountbatten-Windsor Duchess of York, S. (1996). *My Story*. New York: Simon & Schuster.

Finn, N. (2018, January 23). *Best of Both Worlds: How Princess Eugenie and Princess Beatrice Emerged Unscathed From Their Parents' Wild Scandals*. Retrieved from E Online: https://www.eonline.com/ca/news/908306/best-of-both-worlds-how-princess-eugenie-and-princess-beatrice-emerged-unscathed-from-their-parents-wild-scandals

Forsyth, L. (2018, May 2). *'It's not too late!' Meghan Markle's brother*

Thomas pens extraordinary open letter telling Prince Harry 'this is the biggest mistake in royal wedding history' - as he brands his sister 'jaded, shallow and conceited'. Retrieved from Daily Mail: http://www.dailymail.co.uk/news/article-5683559/Meghan-Markles-brother-warns-Prince-Harry-biggest-mistake-royal-wedding-history.html

Foster, M. (2018, May 20). *Royal Reality for Meghan Markle*. Retrieved from Cloutology: https://www.cloutology.com/blog/2018/5/20/royal-reality-and-meghan-markle

Fraser, A., & Holden, M. (2018, May 16). *Meghan Markle's father overshadows her wedding to Prince Harry*. Retrieved from Reuters: https://www.reuters.com/article/us-britain-royals-wedding/meghan-markles-father-overshadows-her-wedding-to-prince-harry-idUSKCN1IH14Z

Friedman, D. (2018, March 7). *How to Cope When Your Friends Are Getting Married and Having Babies, and You Feel Left Behind*. Retrieved from Health.com: http://www.health.com/relationships/coping-friends-life-milestones

Gotyemusic. (2011, July 5). *Gotye - Somebody That I Used To Know (feat. Kimbra) - official video*. Retrieved from YouTube: https://www.youtube.com/watch?v=8UVNT4wvIGY

Green, A. (2018, May 21). *'Do the right thing, Meghan': Royal bride's sister calls on her reunite the family and fly their father to Britain so he can 'fulfil his dream of visiting Buckingham Palace'*. Retrieved from Daily Mail: http://www.dailymail.co.uk/news/article-5755363/Meghans-sister-calls-morally-religiously-right-thing-reunite-family.html

Hains, R. (2016, June 24). *Why Disney princesses and 'princess culture' are bad for girls*. Retrieved from Washington Post:

https://www.washingtonpost.com/posteverything/wp/2016/06/24/princess-culture-is-bad-for-girls-now-theres-proof/?noredirect=on&utm_term=.3d83c09484c8

Halberstam, D. (1971, October 31). *The Vantage Point Perspectives of the Presidency 1963–1969. By Lyndon Baines Johnson. Illustrated. 636 pp. New York: Holt, Rinehart and Winston. $15.* Retrieved from New York Times: https://www.nytimes.com/1971/10/31/archives/the-vantage-point-perspectives-of-the-presidency-19631969-by-lyndon.html

Hall, A. (2016, December 23). *A Brief History Of The Toronto International Film Festival*. Retrieved from Culture Trip: https://theculturetrip.com/north-america/canada/articles/a-brief-history-of-the-toronto-international-film-festival/

Hall, C. (1992, March 29). *Ferige, Andy, Di, and Me*. Retrieved from The Washington Post: https://www.washingtonpost.com/archive/opinions/1992/03/29/fergie-andy-di-and-me/883cb1cd-f4c6-41b6-a055-e59541a2b681/?utm_term=.805fb12a86cb

Hamilton, S. (2017, April 17). *Meghan Markle's partnership with Reitmans comes to an end*. Retrieved from Hello! Canada Magazine: https://ca.hellomagazine.com/royalty/02017041735022/meghan-markle-ends-reitmans-deal

Haniel Vidmar. (2018, March 26). *Interview with HRH Princess of Luxembourg, Tessy Antony*. Retrieved from Haneih Vidmar: http://www.haniehvidmar.com/podcast/interview-with-hrh-princess-of-luxembourg-tessy-antony-part-ii/

Hardy, R. (2017, December 1). *Meghan's maid of honour at her first wedding blames the future Royal for the mysterious end to the marriage: Friend since the age of two describes how fame changed Harry's bride-to-be*. Retrieved from Daily Mail:

http://www.dailymail.co.uk/femail/article-5137785/Meghan-Markle-revelations-friend-knew-best.html

Harvey, S. (2014, October 29). *Everybody that comes with you can't go with you*. Retrieved from Steve Harvey - Twitter: https://twitter.com/iamsteveharvey/status/527639080797229056?lang=en

Hobson, N. (2018, April 23). *The Science of FOMO and What We're Really Missing Out On*. Retrieved from Psychology Today: https://www.psychologytoday.com/ca/blog/ritual-and-the-brain/201804/the-science-fomo-and-what-we-re-really-missing-out

Hodges, T. (2018, May 1). *Long Distance Dating: Are All Long-Distance Relationships Ultimately Doomed?* Retrieved from Ask Men: http://in.askmen.com/doc-love/1091548/article/long-distance-dating

Hola. (2003, September 24). *La verdadera historia de amor de Federico de Dinamarca y Mary Donaldson*. Retrieved from Hola: https://www.hola.com/realeza/casa_danesa/galeria/2003092415247/casasreales/danesa/donaldson/federico1/1/

Holder, M. (2011, August 16). *Saving Sarah: Advice For a Disgraced Duchess*. Retrieved from The Morton Report: http://www.themortonreport.com/celebrity/royals/saving-sarah-advice-for-a-disgraced-duchess/

Holmquist, K. (2010, May 29). *Duchess of the Right Royal Mess*. Retrieved from The Irish Times: https://www.irishtimes.com/life-and-style/people/duchess-of-the-right-royal-mess-1.671752

Home, A. (2009, July 3). *Toxic Workplaces*. Retrieved from Positive Psychology News: http://www.positivepsychologynews.com/news/amanda-horne/200907032876

IMDb.com. (2018, April 25). *I Love Lucy, Quotes, The Black Wig (1954)*. Retrieved from IMDb.com: https://www.imdb.com/title/tt0609344/quotes?item=qt2927987

IMDb.com. (2018, May 2). *Quotes from Gigi, MGM musical*. Retrieved from IMDb.com: https://www.imdb.com/title/tt0051658/quotes

Immaculate Heart High School & Middle School. (2018, May 6). *Campus Ministry & Community Service*. Retrieved from Immaculate Heart High School & Middle School: The Immaculate Heart High School and Middle School. Student Life. Campus Ministry and Community Service. https://www.immaculateheart.org/page/student-life/campus-ministry--community-service

InTouch Weekly. (2018, May 2). *Meghan Markle's Estranged Brother Writes a Letter to Prince Harry (EXCLUSIVE)*. Retrieved from InTouch Weekly: https://www.intouchweekly.com/posts/meghan-markle-brother-prince-harry-letter-159208

Iverem, E. (1988, January 22). *Curious Come For a Glimpse Of Dutchess*. Retrieved from New York Times: https://www.nytimes.com/1988/01/22/nyregion/curious-come-for-a-glimpse-of-dutchess.html

James, W. (2017, April 15). *Prince Harry promises to listen as he starts new Commonwealth job*. Retrieved from Reuters: https://www.reuters.com/article/us-britain-commonwealth-harry/prince-harry-promises-to-listen-as-he-starts-new-commonwealth-job-idUSKBN1HM10N

Jane, E. A. (2018, May 16). *Meghan Markle meet Crown Princess Mary:*

She's been there, done that. Retrieved from ABC News Australia: http://www.abc.net.au/news/2018-05-16/meghan-markle-prince-harry-princess-mary-royal-wedding/9761526

Jefferson, M. (2018, May 5). *No Cinderella: Margo Jefferson on the real Meghan Markle*. Retrieved from The Guardian: https://www.theguardian.com/books/2018/may/05/meghan-markle-royal-wedding-margo-jefferson

Joddle, J. (2015). *The Fetid British Class System*. Retrieved from Jade Joddle Youtube Channel: https://www.youtube.com/watch?v=UOGyx2z6OI

Jones, D. (2018, April 20). *He called her 'the hottest chick in California' and she couldn't keep her hands off him - so, why did Meghan's first marriage to Trevor Engelson implode?* Retrieved from Weekend for Daily Mail: http://www.dailymail.co.uk/femail/article-5625413/Why-did-Meghans-marriage-Trevor-Engelson-implode.html

Jordan, M. (2009, December 20). *With her film 'The Young Victoria," Sarah Ferguson reinvents herself yet again*. Retrieved from The Washington Post: http://www.washingtonpost.com/wp-dyn/content/article/2009/12/18/AR2009121800070_pf.html

Karimi, F. (2017, December 1). *British royals' complicated relationship with Africa*. Retrieved from CNN: https://www.cnn.com/2017/12/01/africa/royals-complicated-relationship-africa/index.html

Kato, M. (2009, May 19). *Weight of Imperial world on Princess Masako: How can former Foreign Ministry star cope with royal straitjacket?* Retrieved from Japan Times: https://www.japantimes.co.jp/news/2009/05/19/reference/weight-of-imperial-world-on-princess-masako/#.WuosqKQvyM8

Kawasaki, G. (2011, October 8). *What I Learned From Steve Jobs*.

Retrieved from Guy Kawasaki: https://guykawasaki.com/what-i-learned-from-steve-jobs/

Kay, R., & Levy, G. (2012, July 27). *Princes at war: How Charles' plans for a slimmed-down monarchy have 'driven a dagger through Andrew's heart' - and sparked a Palace power struggle.* Retrieved from Daily Mail: http://www.dailymail.co.uk/news/article-2180012/Princes-war-How-Charles-plans-slimmed-monarchy-driven-dagger-Andrews-heart--sparked-Palace-power-struggle.html

Kay, R., & Levy, G. (2018, May 16). *Feuding palace courtiers are whispering about the 'Markle debacle' but are they to blame or is it control-freak Harry, asks RICHARD KAY.* Retrieved from Daily Mail: http://www.dailymail.co.uk/news/article-5738059/Courtiers-whispering-Markle-Debacle-arent-blame.html

Kay, R., & Levy, G. (2018, May 5). *Why 'nice but clingy' Harry is marrying Meghan - and not any of his MANY former flames: Prince's complex psychology revealed by Britain's top royal writers.* Retrieved from Mail Online: http://www.dailymail.co.uk/femail/article-5692839/Why-Harrys-marrying-Meghan-not-countless-former-flames.html#ixzz5Ee6iAIoN

Kennedy, D. (1996, December 13). *Three new Sarah Ferguson biographies.* Retrieved from Entertainment Weekly: http://ew.com/article/1996/12/13/three-new-sarah-ferguson-biographies/

Kiefer, E. (2017, May 24). *When Gossiping About Your Girlfriends Is Actually A Good Thing.* Retrieved from Refinery29: https://www.refinery29.com/2017/05/155882/deborah-tannen-interview-women-friendships

Klein Nixon, K. (2018, May16). *AM Show hosts Amanda Gillies and Mark*

Richardson choose sides over Royal Wedding poll. Retrieved from Stuff.co.nz: https://www.stuff.co.nz/entertainment/tv-radio/103937855/am-show-hosts-amanda-gillies-and-mark-richardson-choose-sides-over-royal-wedding-poll

Klein, E. (1993, June 1). *Letter from Tokyo: Masako's Sacrifice (Vanity Fair)*. Retrieved from Edward Klein: http://edwardklein.com/pdfs/june_1993_VF_masakos_sacrifice.pdf

Koubaridis, A. (2018, May 22). *Royal wedding 2018: Meghan Markle's family won't stop causing headaches for the new Duchess of Sussex*. Retrieved from New Zealand Herald: https://www.nzherald.co.nz/lifestyle/news/article.cfm?c_id=6&objectid=12055957

Lam, L. (2018, May 19). *Singapore orchid on Meghan Markle's wedding veil featuring national flowers of Commonwealth countries*. Retrieved from The Straits Times (Singapore): https://www.straitstimes.com/world/singapore-orchid-on-meghan-markles-wedding-veil-featuring-national-flowers-of-commonwealth

Lang, B., & Holmes, M. (2017, February 21). *Yes, Oscars Are a Little Less White — but Hollywood Still Has a Lot of Work to Do*. Retrieved from Variety: http://variety.com/2017/film/awards/oscar-diversity-hollywood-women-minorities-1201992208/

Lashinsky, A. (2017, May 26). *Mark Zuckerberg's Good Idea*. Retrieved from Fortune Magazine: http://fortune.com/2017/05/26/mark-zuckerbergs-good-idea/

Levy, G. a. (2011, June 29). *http://www.dailymail.co.uk/femail/article-2009312/Finding-Sarah-Duchess-Yorks-book-airbrushed-cover.html*. Retrieved from Daily Mail: http://www.dailymail.co.uk/femail/article-2009312/Finding-Sarah-Duchess-Yorks-book-airbrushed-cover.html#ixzz5DXsFhsu3

Linning, S. (2014, August 9). *Sarah Ferguson to cut short Balmoral break with Prince Andrew and the Queen before Prince Philip arrives because he 'won't have her in the house'.* Retrieved from Daily Mail: http://www.dailymail.co.uk/news/article-2720527/Sarah-Ferguson-cut-short-Balmoral-break-Prince-Andrew-Queen-Prince-Philip-arrives-wont-house.html

Little Black Dress. (2017, November 22). *In Conversation with. . .a Princess.* Retrieved from Little Black Dress: https://www.littleblackdress.co.uk/magazine/fashion-fix/princess-tessy/

Loverboy. (2018, May 2). *Loverboy 1980 album.* Retrieved from Loverboy: http://www.loverboyband.com/js_albums/loverboy-1980/

Lusher, A. (2018, May 15). *Huge drop in number of royal wedding street parties compared to Will and Kate's big day.* Retrieved from The Independent: https://www.independent.co.uk/news/uk/home-news/royal-wedding-street-parties-meghan-markle-prince-harry-not-interested-yougov-poll-will-kate-a8352386.html

Lusher, A. (2018, May 16). *Is Thomas Markle's story of whether to attend the royal wedding a 'rollercoaster of speculation' or a cruel soap opera?* Retrieved from The Independent: https://www.independent.co.uk/news/uk/home-news/thomas-markle-meghan-father-royal-wedding-prince-harry-media-tmz-latest-attend-walk-down-aisle-a8354376.html

Mahon, E. K. (2008, March 5). *Sarah, Duchess of York.* Retrieved from Scandalous Women: http://scandalouswoman.blogspot.com/2008/03/sarah-duchess-of-york.html

Malkin, B. (2011, June 9). *Sarah Ferguson's sister says she doesn't recall any abuse*. Retrieved from The Daily Telegraph: https://www.telegraph.co.uk/news/uknews/theroyalfamily/8565967/Sarah-Fergusons-sister-says-she-doesnt-recall-any-abuse.html

Maloney, M. (2018, May 4). *How Meghan Markle's Parents' Roles in the Royal Wedding Differ From Kate Middleton's Parents*. Retrieved from Town and Country: https://www.townandcountrymag.com/society/tradition/a20154007/meghan-markle-kate-middleton-parents-roles-in-royal-wedding-comparison/

Marche, S. (2016, July 4). *Welcome to the new Toronto: the most fascinatingly boring city in the world*. Retrieved from The Guardian: https://www.theguardian.com/cities/2016/jul/04/new-toronto-most-fascinatingly-boring-city-guardian-canada-week

Marikar, S. (2011, May 11). *Sarah Ferguson Opens Up About Royal Wedding Rejection on 'Oprah'*. Retrieved from ABC News.com: https://abcnews.go.com/Entertainment/sarah-ferguson-opens-royal-wedding-rejection-oprah/story?id=13579087

Maxtone Graham, Y. (2018, May 17). *Does Harry need a wife or a mother? Diana's death left her younger son in 'chaos'. An author who had exclusive access to the Prince says Meghan gives him the maternal nurturing he needs*. Retrieved from Daily Mail: http://www.dailymail.co.uk/home/books/article-5742173/Does-Harry-need-wife-mother.html#ixzz5FoxqV8MW

McDonaugh, M. (2010, May 24). *It's Fergie's stupidity and self-delusion that sum her up*. Retrieved from Daily Telegraph: https://www.telegraph.co.uk/news/uknews/theroyalfamily/7758143/Its-Fergies-stupidity-and-self-denial-that-sum-her-up.html

Mellado, A. (2019, January 13). *Tessy de Luxemburgo: «Un divorcio siempre es difícil, pero hay que adaptarse»*. Retrieved from ABC

Gente y Estilo: http://www.abc.es/estilo/gente/abci-tessy-luxemburgo-divorcio-siempre-dificil-pero-adaptarse-201801130143_noticia.html

Merrick, J. (2018, May 16). *The paparazzi Prince Harry fears is back -- just in time for his wedding.* Retrieved from CNN: https://edition.cnn.com/2018/05/15/opinions/meghan-markle-dad-vilified-for-being-american-merrick-opinion-intl/index.html

Milburn, A. (2017, November 28). *Social mobility is a stark postcode lottery. Too many in Britain are being left behind.* Retrieved from The Guardian: https://www.theguardian.com/inequality/2017/nov/28/social-mobility-stark-postcode-lottery-too-many-britain-left-behind-alan-milburn-commission-report

Millar, J. (2018, May 18). *Prince Charles saves the day: Meghan Markle to walk down aisle with new father-in-law.* Retrieved from Daily Express: https://www.express.co.uk/news/royal/961576/Meghan-Markle-aisle-Prince-Charles-royal-wedding-2018-latest-news

Mills, S. (2018, May 6). *Meghan Markle has new role to master: British royal protocol.* Retrieved from Reuters: https://www.reuters.com/article/us-britain-royals-protocol/meghan-markle-has-new-role-to-master-british-royal-protocol-idUSKBN1I800B

Moir, J. (2009, October 15). *At 50 the Duchess of York is still a Woman Who Never Learns.* Retrieved from Daily Mail: http://www.dailymail.co.uk/debate/article-1220496/At-50-Duchess-York-woman-learns.html

Mooney, S., & Linning, S. (2017, January 18). *'Extremely sad' Princess Tessy, 31, of Luxembourg announces she is divorcing husband Prince Louis, 30, after 10 years of marriage in first high-profile European royal divorce in more than a decade.* Retrieved from

Daily Mail: http://www.dailymail.co.uk/femail/article-4133166/Princess-Tessy-Luxembourg-divorcing-Prince-Louis.html

Moore, S. (2018, May 3). *I wouldn't go to Harry and Meghan's pay-as-you-go bash. It's pure meanness.* Retrieved from The Guardian: https://www.theguardian.com/commentisfree/2018/may/03/harry-meghan-pay-as-you-go-wedding-commoners-royal-wedding

Morgan, P. (2018, May 21). *Dear Meghan, congrats on a brilliant Season 1 finale, but trust me, Season 2 will be a hundred times tougher if you start lecturing us about sexual equality from your servant-laden Palace.* Retrieved from Daily Mail: http://www.dailymail.co.uk/news/article-5753647/PIERS-MORGAN-Congrats-Meghan-tough-start-lecturing-equality-palace.html

Morgan, P. (2018, May 16). *Why Meghan, Harry and the clueless Palace may come to rue the day they left the backstabbing, money-grabbing Markles out in the cold and turned this wedding into a right royal tacky mess.* Retrieved from Daily Mail: http://www.dailymail.co.uk/news/article-5736007/PIERS-MORGAN-Meghan-Harry-Palace-rue-day-left-Markles-cold.html

Morton, A. (2018). *Meghan: A Hollywood Princess.* New York: Grand Central Publishing .

Morton, A. (2018, May 16). *The Meghan Markle paradox: Andrew Morton explores how a modern woman can fit the mould of an ancient tradition.* Retrieved from The Globe and Mail (Toronto): https://www.theglobeandmail.com/opinion/article-the-meghan-paradox-how-can-a-modern-woman-fit-the-mould-of-ancient/

Morton, A. (2018, May 2). *The things I've learnt about Meghan Markle, by her unofficial royal biographer.* Retrieved from Town and

Country: http://www.tatler.com/article/royal-biographer-andrew-morton-on-meghan-markle-interview

Mount, H. (2017, December 9). *Harry, Meghan and the irresistible rise of the glamocracy*. Retrieved from The Spectator: https://www.spectator.co.uk/2017/12/harry-meghan-and-the-irresistible-rise-of-the-glamocracy/

Murphy, J. (2017, November 27). *Meghan Markle and her life among Toronto 'royalty'*. Retrieved from BBC: http://www.bbc.com/news/world-us-canada-41768867

National Portrait Gallery UK. (2018, May 10). *Princess Marina, Duchess of Kent (1906-1968)*. Retrieved from National Portrait Gallery UK: https://www.npg.org.uk/collections/search/person/mp05475/princess-marina-duchess-of-kent

Naylor, T. (2018, May 17). *From the royal wedding menu to Nigella – why bowl food is so wildly popular*. Retrieved from The Guardian: https://www.theguardian.com/lifeandstyle/2018/may/17/royal-wedding-menu-nigella-bowl-food-instagram-craze-meghan-harry

news.com.au. (2018, April 17). *Prince Harry gets new role as Commonwealth Youth Ambassador*. Retrieved from News.com.au: http://www.news.com.au/entertainment/celebrity-life/royals/prince-harry-gets-new-role-as-commonwealth-youth-ambassador/news-story/2b2b68c7bfde8969d4dabf2864f5af92

Newsweek. (1996, October 13). *ROYAL BLUSH*. Retrieved from Newsweek: http://www.newsweek.com/royal-blush-179280

Nordell, J. (2018, April 26). *How Slack Got Ahead in Diversity*. Retrieved from The Atlantic: https://www.theatlantic.com/technology/archive/2018/04/how-slack-got-ahead-in-diversity/558806/

Norman, J., & Iggulden, T. (2015, November 15). *Knights and dames scrapped from Order of Australia, Malcolm Turnbull says*. Retrieved from ABC News Australia: http://www.abc.net.au/news/2015-11-02/knights-and-dames-to-be-scrapped/6904474

O'Connor, T. (2018, May 16). *How to Dress Meghan Markle (Hint: You Probably Can't)*. Retrieved from Business of Fashion: https://www.businessoffashion.com/articles/intelligence/the-challenges-of-dressing-meghan-markle

Oppenheim, M. (2018, April 28). *Ann Widdecombe attacks Prince Harry and Meghan Markle for supporting LGBT+ rights*. Retrieved from The Independent: https://www.independent.co.uk/news/uk/home-news/ann-widdecombe-meghan-markle-lgbt-rights-prince-harry-royal-wedding-a8323486.html

Oprah Winfrey Network. (2011, May 3). *Finding Sarah - First Look: Finding Sarah - Premieres Sunday, June 12th at 9/8c*. Retrieved from Oprah Winfrey Network: http://www.oprah.com/own/first-look-finding-sarah-own-tv

Oprah Winfrey Show. (2011, May 3). *Finding Sarah Ferguson*. Retrieved from Oprah Winfrey Show: http://www.oprah.com/oprahshow/finding-sarah-ferguson/all

Order of Splendour. (2011, September 28). *Wedding Wednesday: Louis and Tessy's Wedding*. Retrieved from Order of Splendour: http://orderofsplendor.blogspot.com/2011/09/wedding-wednesday-louis-and-tessys.html

Palmo, R. (2006, September 30). *The Windsor-Rome Reunion*. Retrieved from Whispers in the Loggia blog: http://whispersintheloggia.blogspot.com/2006/09/windsor-rome-reunion.html

Paras, P. (2018, February 27). *Meet the First European Princess of African Descent, Angela of Liechtenstein*. Retrieved from Town & Country: https://www.townandcountry.ph/people/heritage/princess-angela-of-liechtenstein-facts-a1867-20180227-lfrm

Park LaBrea News Beverly Press. (2017, November 30). *Immaculate Heart alumna Meghan Markle announces engagement to Prince Harry*. Retrieved from Beverly Press: http://beverlypress.com/2017/11/immaculate-heart-alumna-meghan-markle-announces-engagement-to-prince-harry/

Parker, A. (2015, December 29). *Jeb Bush Sprints to Escape Donald Trump's 'Low Energy' Label*. Retrieved from New York Times: https://www.nytimes.com/2015/12/30/us/politics/jeb-bush-sprints-to-escape-donald-trumps-low-energy-label.html

Perrring, R. (2018, May 3). *How Sarah Ferguson was SHUT OUT of Royal Family - 'There was Fergie in a shocking scene'*. Retrieved from Daily Express: https://www.express.co.uk/news/royal/954214/Sarah-ferguson-fergie-latest-royal-family-toe-sucking-scandal

Pickhardt, C. E. (2010, December 13). *Adolescence and the Case of Odd Parent Out*. Retrieved from Psychology Today: https://www.psychologytoday.com/us/blog/surviving-your-childs-adolescence/201012/adolescence-and-the-case-odd-parent-out

Platell, A. (2018, April 20). *Platell's People: Don't too grand for your own family, Meghan...it says more about you than about them*. Retrieved from Daily Mail: http://www.dailymail.co.uk/debate/article-5640741/Platells-

People-Dont-grand-family-Meghan.html

Price, L., & Logan, H. (2014, June 19). *Lloyd Price - Personality*. Retrieved from YouTube: https://www.youtube.com/watch?v=W2aD25M5Su8

Pukas, A. (2007, March 15). *Forever the royal outcast*. Retrieved from Daily Express: https://www.express.co.uk/expressyourself/2273/Forever-the-royal-outcast

Quinn Association. (2018, May 5). *Robert E. Quinn's Competing Values Framework*. Retrieved from Quinn Association: https://www.quinnassociation.com/en/robert_e_quinns_competing_values_framework

Quinn, R. E., & Rohrbaugh, J. (1983). A Spatial Model of Effectiveness Criteria: Towards a Competing Values Approach to Organizational Analysis. *Management Science*, 363-377. Retrieved from http://www.valuebasedmanagement.net/methods_quinn_competing_values_framework.html

Radio Times. (2015, February 19). *Reinventing the Royals: spin in the house of Windsor*. Retrieved from Radio Times: http://www.radiotimes.com/news/2015-02-19/reinventing-the-royals-spin-in-the-house-of-windsor/

Rankin, J. (2017, December 28). *'A special place for Luxembourgish': Grand Duchy's native language enjoys renaissance*. Retrieved from The Guardian: https://www.theguardian.com/world/2017/dec/28/luxembourgish-grand-duchys-native-language-enjoys-renaissance

Reilly, K. (2017, November 27). *Read About Prince Harry and Meghan Markle's Sweet First Date in Their Post-Engagement Interview*. Retrieved from Time.com: http://time.com/5038618/prince-harry-meghan-markle-engaged-bbc-interview-transcript/

Ritschel, C. (2018, May 3). *Meghan Markle's brother says it is not 'too late' to call off the wedding in letter to Prince Harry*. Retrieved from The Independent: https://www.independent.co.uk/royalwedding/meghan-markle-brother-letter-thomas-markle-jr-estranged-prince-harry-a8333676.html

Robertson, L. (2018, April 29). *Why Learn about your enneagram type*. Retrieved from Nine Rivers Wellness: http://nineriverswellness.com/why-learn-about-your-enneagram-type-2

Rodger, J. (2017, March 15). *JoJo Bows are sweeping the UK and being BANNED - and here's why*. Retrieved from Birmingham Mail: https://www.birminghammail.co.uk/whats-on/family-kids-news/jojo-bows-latest-trend-hit-12639417

Rose, C., & Nicholl, M. (1996). *Accelerated Learning for the 21st Century*. London: Piatkus.

Roseman, D. (1996, April 20). *Is this the day when royalty lost the plot?* Retrieved from The Independent: https://www.independent.co.uk/news/uk/home-news/was-this-the-day-when-royalty-lost-the-plot-1305932.html

Royal House of Norway. (2017, January 15). *Her Royal Highness Crown Princess Mette-Marit*. Retrieved from Royal House of Norway: http://www.royalcourt.no/artikkel.html?tid=28772&sek=28635

Royal House of Norway. (2017, August 29). *His Royal Highness Crown Prince Haakon*. Retrieved from Royal House of Norway: http://www.royalcourt.no/artikkel.html?tid=28766&sek=28640

RTL.be. (2017, Nov 25). *Princesse Tessy: sa nouvelle vie celibataire - Place Royale*. Retrieved from RTL.be:

https://www.rtl.be/info/video/651063.aspx

RTL.lu. (2017, Oct 27). *La Princesse Tessy se confie sur son divorce*. Retrieved from RTL.lu: http://5minutes.rtl.lu/grande-region/luxembourg/1089606.html

Rudulph, H. W. (2017, October 11). *How Women Talk: Heather Wood Rudulph Interviews Deborah Tannen*. Retrieved from LA Review of Books: https://lareviewofbooks.org/article/how-women-talk-heather-wood-rudulph-interviews-deborah-tannen/#!

Ruhlmann, W. (2018, May 2). *album review of Crash by Human League*. Retrieved from All Music: https://www.allmusic.com/album/crash-mw0000190358

Salens, R. (2014, May 17). *Louis et Tessy de Luxembourg : diplômés de l'université à Londres*. Retrieved from Nobleese et Royautes: http://www.noblesseetroyautes.com/louis-et-tessy-de-luxembourg-diplomes-de-luniversite-a-londres/

Salens, R. (2018, May 6). *Le prince Jean-Christophe Napoléon aux Invalides*. Retrieved from Noblesse et Royautes: http://www.noblesseetroyautes.com/147820-2/

Sales, N. J. (2011, May 19). *Sarah Ferguson: The Real Story*. Retrieved from Harper's Bazaar: https://www.harpersbazaar.com/celebrity/latest/news/a728/sarah-ferguson-interview/

Samuelson, K. (2017, November 28). *From Wildcat to royalty. 2003 Northwestern graduate Meghan Markle to marry Prince Harry*. Retrieved from Northwestern University: https://news.northwestern.edu/stories/2017/november/from-wildcat-to-royalty/

Sawer, P. (2017, October 14). *Princess of Luxembourg branded 'gold digger' as she takes divorce to UK court*. Retrieved from The

Telegraph: https://www.telegraph.co.uk/news/2017/10/14/princess-branded-gold-digger-takes-divorce-uk-court/

Schwartz, B. (2013, November 23). *The Tender Letter Queen Elizabeth's Father Wrote to Her On Her Wedding Day Will Make You Misty*. Retrieved from Redbook: https://www.redbookmag.com/life/news/a41100/king-george-letter-queen-elizabeth-wedding/

Scotto Di Santolo, A. (2018, May 18). *Royal commentator WARNS Royal Family could become the 'British Kardashians'*. Retrieved from Daily Express: https://www.express.co.uk/news/royal/961690/Royal-Wedding-2018-Kardashians-Royal-Family-Meghan-Markle-Prince-Harry

Sharma, G. (2008, May 28). *Nepal abolishes centuries-old Hindu monarchy*. Retrieved from Reuters: https://www.reuters.com/article/us-nepal-king/nepal-abolishes-centuries-old-hindu-monarchy-idUSISL5996320080529

Shreenan, P. (2011, September 1). *At Wit's End - Shift to the Gift: Know Yourself! Angry? Sad? Suspicious?* Retrieved from At Wits End: www.at_wits_end.islandnet.com

Sister Patricia Shreenan, S. (2018, May 13). Interview with Enneagram teacher, Sister Patricia Shreenan. (J. Seto, Interviewer)

Smith, M. C., & Turner, S. (2015, May 12). *The Radical Transformation of Diversity and Inclusion (Deloitte)*. Retrieved from Deloitte: https://www2.deloitte.com/us/en/pages/about-deloitte/articles/radical-transformation-of-diversity-and-inclusion.html

Spector, F. (2018, March 29). *Sarah Ferguson: Meghan Markle is 'the

SAME' as Duchess of York, insists royal source. Retrieved from Daily Express: https://www.express.co.uk/life-style/life/938438/sarah-ferguson-meghan-markle-duchess-of-york-fergie-the-same

Spoto, D. (2009). *High Society: The Life of Grace Kelly.* New York: Three Rivers Press.

Stanley, A. (2011, June 9). *You Can Feel Her Pain (Just Don't Ask Questions).* Retrieved from The New York Times: https://www.nytimes.com/2011/06/10/arts/television/finding-sarah-with-sarah-ferguson-on-own-review.html

Starkie, A. (1996). *Fergie: Her Secret Life.* London: Michael O'Mara Books.

Steafel, E. (2018, May 16). *The makings of the Markle debacle - how a simmering family feud came to a head at the royal wedding.* Retrieved from Daily Telegraph: https://www.telegraph.co.uk/news/2018/05/16/makings-markle-debacle-family-feud-almost-derailed-royal-wedding/

Sternberg, R. J. (2014, January 27). *Coping With a Career Crisis.* Retrieved from The Chronicle of Higher Education: https://www.chronicle.com/article/Coping-With-a-Career-Crisis/144191

Stickings, T., & English, R. (2018, May 18). *Stand By Me, gospel choir, alternate vows and VERY modern Order of Service (but they didn't have time to delete bride's absent dad): Everything you need to know about Harry and Meghan's wedding.* Retrieved from Mail Online: http://www.dailymail.co.uk/news/article-5746781/Harry-Meghans-modern-Order-Service.html

Sykes, T. (2018, May 15). *How TMZ Crashed Meghan Markle and Prince Harry's Wedding. Devastatingly.* Retrieved from Daily Beast: https://www.thedailybeast.com/how-tmz-crashed-meghan-markle-and-prince-harrys-wedding-devastatingly

Sykes, T. (2018, May 17). *Meghan Markle Can Help the Royal Family Change—If It Wants To*. Retrieved from Daily Beast: https://www.thedailybeast.com/meghan-markle-can-help-the-royal-family-changeif-it-wants-to?ref=author

Sykes, T. (2018, February 12). *The Rehabilitation of Fergie, the Comeback Duchess*. Retrieved from Daily Beast: https://www.thedailybeast.com/the-rehabilitation-of-fergie-the-comeback-duchess?ref=scroll

Szklarski, C. (2018, May 10). *'We kind of adopted her': Toronto royal fans embrace Meghan Markle*. Retrieved from CTV News, The Canadian Press: https://www.ctvnews.ca/mobile/world/the-royals/we-kind-of-adopted-her-toronto-royal-fans-embrace-meghan-markle-1.3922394

Tessy, H. P. (2016, October 1). *Princess Tessy of Luxembourg on serving in a warzone and being a victim of attempted abuse*. Retrieved from Daily Telegraph: https://www.telegraph.co.uk/women/life/princess-tessy-of-luxembourg-on-serving-in-a-warzone-and-being-a/

The CyberHymnal. (2017, December 12). *Keep on the Sunny Side of Life*. Retrieved from Hymn Time: http://www.hymntime.com/tch/htm/k/e/e/keesunny.htm

The Futon Critic. (2010, August 24). *Breaking News: Development Update: Tuesday, August 24*. Retrieved from The Futon Critic: http://www.thefutoncritic.com/news/2010/08/24/development-update-tuesday-august-24-37122/8850/

The Governor General of Canada. (2018, May 10). *Former Governor General: Edward Richard Schreyer*. Retrieved from The Governor General of Canada: http://www.gg.ca/document.aspx?lan=eng&id=15233

Tilsner, J. (1995). Pigeonholing goes corporate: American business is using the Enneagram of Personality types, Oct 10, 1995. *Business Week*, 23.

TMZ. (2018, May 18). *I'm Honored Prince Charles Will Walk You Down the Aisle!!!* Retrieved from TMZ.com: http://www.tmz.com/2018/05/18/meghan-markle-prince-harry-charles-down-aisle-thomas-dad-proud/

TMZ. (2018, May 16). *You Can't Censor me, Meghn... I'm an American!!!* Retrieved from TMZ: http://www.tmz.com/2018/05/16/samantha-meghan-markle-half-sister-royal-wedding-talking-america/

Toronto Life. (2018, April 27). *What we learned about Meghan Markle's time in Toronto from a new biography of her*. Retrieved from Toronto Life: https://torontolife.com/city/life/learned-meghan-markles-time-toronto-new-biography/

Treble, P. (2018, May 15). *Who's to blame for the Thomas Markle fiasco?* Retrieved from Maclean's: https://www.macleans.ca/royalty/whos-to-blame-for-the-thomas-markle-fiasco/

Trooper. (2018, May 2). *Knock em dead, kid album by Trooper*. Retrieved from Trooper: http://www.trooper.com/index.php?page=album3

Troy-Pryde, J. (2017, June 14). *Was Prince Charles 'jealous' of William following his wedding to Kate?* Retrieved from Marie Claire: http://www.marieclaire.co.uk/news/celebrity-news/prince-charles-jealous-william-514678

Tweedie, N. (2005, February 11). *Charles and Camilla, after Diana*. Retrieved from Daily Telegraph: https://www.telegraph.co.uk/news/uknews/1483284/Charles-and-Camilla-after-Diana.html

UNA-UK. (2017, March 23). *A conversation with Princess Tessy, UNA-UK Patron*. Retrieved from UNA-UK: https://www.una.org.uk/magazine/1-2017/conversation-princess-tessy-una-uk-patron

US Weekly staff. (2011, May 10). *Sarah Ferguson: Royal Wedding Snub "Was So Difficult"*. Retrieved from US Weekly: https://www.usmagazine.com/celebrity-news/news/sarah-ferguson-royal-wedding-snub-was-so-difficult-2011105/

Vickers, H. (2003, March 18). *Obituary: Major Ronald Ferguson*. Retrieved from The Independent: https://www.independent.co.uk/news/obituaries/major-ronald-ferguson-36350.html

Vulpo, M. (2018, May 19). *Why Sarah Ferguson's Appearance at the Royal Wedding Is So Significant*. Retrieved from E Online: https://www.eonline.com/ca/news/937067/why-sarah-ferguson-s-appearance-at-the-royal-wedding-is-so-significant

Wallace, C. (1986, August 4). *The Royal Wedding*. Retrieved from People Magazine: http://people.com/archive/cover-story-the-royal-wedding-vol-26-no-5/

Ward, V. (2010, November 21). *Royal Wedding: Bishop predicts Prince William's marriage to Kate Middleton will only last seven years*. Retrieved from Daily Telegraph: https://www.telegraph.co.uk/news/uknews/royal-wedding/8149637/Royal-Wedding-Bishop-predicts-Prince-Williams-marriage-to-Kate-Middleton-will-only-last-seven-years.html

Watson, S. (2018, May 4). *The pre-nup clean-up: why Harry's wedding diet and style make-over isn't a cause for celebration* . Retrieved from Daily Telegraph: https://www.telegraph.co.uk/men/relationships/pre-nup-clean-up-harrys-wedding-diet-style-make-over-bad-news/

Watt, H., Pegg, D., Garside, J., & Bengtsson, H. (2016, April 6). *From Kubrick to Cowell: Panama Papers expose offshore dealings of the stars*. Retrieved from The Guardian: https://www.theguardian.com/news/2016/apr/06/panama-papers-reveal-offshore-dealings-stars

Weber, P. (2017, October 20). *Dossier royal: on vous dit tout sur les raisons taboues du divorce du prince Louis et de Tessy de Luxembourg*. Retrieved from RTL Belge: https://www.rtl.be/people/potins/le-divorce-du-prince-louis-et-de-tessy-de-luxembourg-les-raisons-sont-taboues-963368.aspx

Weiji, C. (2016, May 16). *When people set big goals for themselves and try to become successful, why are they sometimes mocked, doubted, and discouraged by their friends, coworkers, and relatives?* Retrieved from Quora: https://www.quora.com/When-people-set-big-goals-for-themselves-and-try-to-become-successful-why-are-they-sometimes-mocked-doubted-and-discouraged-by-their-friends-coworkers-and-relatives/answer/Clay-Weiji

Widdecombe, A. (2018, April 25). *Meghan Markle will be a breath of fresh air in a stuffy family, says ANN WIDDECOMBE*. Retrieved from Daily Express: https://www.express.co.uk/comment/columnists/ann-widdecombe/951017/meghan-markle-royal-family-popular-ann-widdecombe

Wilcox, Q. (2014, June 17). *Trailing Spouse vs. Accompanying Spouse: Semantics or Principle?* Retrieved from Huffington Post: https://www.huffingtonpost.com/quenby-wilcox-/trailing-spouse-vs-accompanying-spouse_b_5163777.html

Williams, J. T. (1998, Winter). *The Future of the British Monarchy*. Retrieved from Interstate: Journal of International Affairs: https://interstate1965.wordpress.com/archives/19981999-

issue-1/the-future-of-the-british-monarchy/

Wilson, C. (2007, February 12). *What this picture tells us about Fergie*. Retrieved from Daily Mail: http://www.dailymail.co.uk/tvshowbiz/article-435784/What-picture-tells-Fergie.html

Yossman, K. (2018, May 3). *For Meghan Markle, playing a princess carries some risks. Is this L.A. girl up to it?* Retrieved from Los Angeles Times: http://www.latimes.com/fashion/la-ig-british-royal-wedding-fashion-meghan-markle-20180503-htmlstory.html

Youtube. (2012, July 17). *Don't Fence Me in Dean Martin and Lorne Greene - The Dean Martin Show*. Retrieved from Youtube: https://www.youtube.com/watch?v=hlHb8fIjJ4Y

Zillman, C., & Fry, E. (2018, February 18). *HR Is Not Your Friend. Here's Why*. Retrieved from Fortune: http://fortune.com/2018/02/16/microsoft-hr-problem-metoo/

ABOUT THE AUTHOR
JANICE SETO

Janice Seto writes non-fiction and commentary including articles for The Bridge, the publication of The Malaysia-Canada Business Council. *Save Your Breath: Making Better Deals by Talking Less* is an expansion on her article, on negotiating, for The Bridge.

Over the years, she has studied royalty and studied the Enneagram personality system and written her dissertation on the topic. Royalty Meets Enneagram is her latest series.

Her more recent books are also available on Amazon: *Standing Out in The Background – A Guide to Extra Work in Toronto's Film & TV Industry* and *Johnny Seto's Bowmanville – An Enneagram Perspective*.

Her first children's book, *Walking for Clean Water: Pukatawagan on the Move*, is in English and Cree, with Ralph Caribou providing the Rock Cree dialect translation.

The System for Women is her first book series on relationships, based on the hilarious but insightful work of Doc Love http://www.doclove.com/. Parts 1 and 3 reached #2 on the Amazon Bestseller list in its category as a free download. Part 5: Pride and Prejudice reached #1.

Bowmanville's Octagon House – From Church and Faith and Tait to Irwin & Seto also went all the way to #1.

http://janiceseto.wix.com/words
amazon.com/author/janiceseto
www.janiceseto.com

The System for Her

Adapting the wisdom of DocLove with examples from the over 130 Harlequin/Mills & Boon books by Betty Neels, Janice Seto's The System for Her series provides clear insight into the mysterious behaviour of women and men in pursuit of their Happily Ever After.

Part 1: Doc Love Lessons in Betty Neels Books

The System for Her, Part 1: Doc Love Lessons from Betty Neels books shows how extensive research by Doc Love (www.doclove.com) into successful relationships takes shape in the gentlemen and the ladies in the Harlequin/Mills & Boon books by Mrs. Neels - and these translate into timeless lessons for today's modern reader.
https://www.amazon.com/System-Her-Part-Lessons-Betty/dp/1926935225

Part 2: Doc Love Lessons in Betty Neels Heroes

In this second book on relationships inspired by Doc Love, this time author Janice Seto puts the men in Betty Neels romances under the microscope. The System for Women, Part 2: Doc Love Lessons in Betty Neels Heroes introduces you to the ideal hero, the Gentleman and his hangers-on that include the Macho Boy, the Teddy Bear, the Wimpus Americanus.
https://www.amazon.com/System-Her-Part-Lessons-Heroes/dp/1926935241/

Part 3: Doc Love Lessons in Betty Neels Heroines

In this third book on relationships inspired by DocLove, Janice Seto uncovers key nuggets of female happiness. *The System for Women, Part 3: Doc Love Lessons in Betty Neels Heroines*, keeps it simple. Bid good-bye to Blockers, Veronicas, and embrace your timesaving Reality Factors and The Bottom Line.
https://www.amazon.com/System-Her-Part-Lessons-Heroines/dp/1926935268/

Part 4: Doc Love Lessons in Betty Neels Happily Ever After

In this fourth book on relationships inspired by DocLove, Janice Seto looks past 'I do'. The System for Women, Part 4: Doc Love Lessons in Betty Neels Happily Ever After lays out Doc Love's Maintenance Program for keeping Ms Right in love. The author also reveals the three Black Swans of a hell-on-earth relationship. This book is a must for the couple who truly wants to live Happily Ever After.
https://www.amazon.com/System-Lessons-Betty-Neels-Happily/dp/1926935284/

Royalty Meets Enneagram

In this series on royal figures based on the Enneagram typology system, Janice Seto has a lighthearted look into their distinct personalities.

Based on years of research, she says their behaviours and actions and portrayals in the media emanate from one of 9 personality styles. For royal watchers everywhere as the series looks at European as well as the British royals.

Enneagram 7 Promoter Princess: Meghan Markle, Sarah Ferguson, Princess Tessy

What do Meghan Markle, Sarah Ferguson Duchess of York, and Tessy de Nassau, Princess of Luxembourg (Antony) have in common? It may be their personality styles!

Enneagram 7 Promoter Princess personalities are known for their effervescent energy, fun frolics, and optimistic outlook. Sure, there are pitfalls that come with the package, but you can't take your eyes (or paparazzi lens) off of them!